The Next
Greatest
Thing
50
YEARS
1935
1985
RURAL ELECTRIFICATION

"Brothers and sisters,
I want to tell you this.
The greatest thing on earth
is to have the love of God in your
heart, and the next greatest thing
is to have electricity
in your house."

Farmer giving witness in a rural Tennessee church in the early 1940s

THE NEXT GREATEST THING

RICHARD A. PENCE
Editor

PATRICK DAHL
Consulting Editor

JANE CRAWFORD
Designer

HARLAN M. SEVERSON
Rural Electrification Administration
Editorial Advisor

ANN LUPPI
Research and Production Associate

SOCORRO Q. GONZÁLEZ
Artist

♦

THE NATIONAL RURAL ELECTRIC COOPERATIVE ASSOCIATION
WASHINGTON, DC

This publication was authorized by the
Board of Directors of the National Rural Electric
Cooperative Association and published by the Public & Association
Affairs Department of NRECA.

The National Rural Electric Cooperative Association was organized in 1942 to provide legislative, communications, insurance, management and other services to the more than 1,000 rural electric cooperatives which provide electric power to much of the rural areas of the United States. The Association's membership includes distribution cooperatives or other nonprofit consumer-owned rural electric utilities, generation and transmission cooperatives, and other nonprofit associations providing services to them. Other allied organizations, such as credit unions for rural electric employees, are affiliate nonvoting members.

THE NEXT GREATEST THING

First Printing, October, 1984
Second Printing, April, 1985
Third Printing, March, 1993

Library of Congress Catalog Card Number: 84-60901

ISBN 0-917599-00-4

Printed by union printers at Colortone Press, Washington, DC, U.S.A.

To the founders and pioneers of rural electrification, who—with grit, sweat and vision—transformed rural America from the depths of despair and darkness to the splendor of hope and light, and who serve as our reminder that no job is too tough if the cause is just and the people are determined.

Preface

More than three years ago, staff members here at the National Rural Electric Cooperative Association began to discuss ways to commemorate in 1985 the 50th anniversary of the Rural Electrification Administration. Out of those discussions came the conviction that the celebration called for some sort of enduring "centerpiece" to honor this most-loved government program among rural people. We conceived this book as that lasting tribute.

Our intent has been to reflect the special feeling many rural people have for "the REA," which provided them with the vehicle for eliminating darkness and drudgery. Every rural American carries an individual testimony to the significance of electricity in his or her daily life, whether in an historical context of how it was before electricity, or out of present-day reflections on how life would be without it. This book seeks to serve as a testament of each individual's personal experience and, beyond that, as a collective remembrance.

In these pages we share the discoveries made during three years of unstinting searches in the "dust and must" of REA publications and documents, the National Archives, the Library of Congress, state historical societies, institutional and city archives, presidential and university libraries, the files of NRECA and its members, and the scrapbooks and personal memories of many REA and co-op veterans.

Our goal throughout this effort was to find the most telling photographs and facts about rural electrification. The quest turned up an almost limitless supply of both. Not always were the photos of the quality we would have preferred; sometimes we had to use a technically inferior photo because it told the "right" story. But the best of these—technically, artistically and "humanly"—are woven together to tell the magnificent and enduring story of how rural America "got lights."

The result transcends the mere technical achievement of electrifying the countryside to become a moving documentary of how rural Americans, in partnership with their federal government, joined together to improve their lives and the lives of succeeding generations.

That it does this is largely due to the efforts of Patrick Dahl, who poured heart and soul into every page. It was primarily he who relentlessly pursued every clue in discovering bits of history in and about the photos. And it was he who crafted most of the words between these covers. In all of this, he greatly enhances his reputation of knowing—or being able to find out—everything relating to rural electrification.

Jane Crawford gave beauty and continuity to the pages through her design and art direction. Her devotion to this book and to the rural electrification program itself buoyed our staff throughout the project. Her assistant, Socorro (Sokie) Q. Gonzalez, masterfully illustrated the photographs, executing the layout art for the printers with exquisitely detailed drawings.

Ann Luppi made herself invaluable, particularly with the pre-REA archives research, and by being the "glue" during the pressures of production. Her insights made this book much less parochial than it otherwise might have been.

All of us are indebted to many people for their help and cooperation in making this book a reality.

Our appreciation goes to Harold Hunter, administrator of the Rural Electrification Administration, and the members of his staff for their support. We especially thank Mr. Hunter for allowing us to "borrow" Harlan Severson during the conception and organization of the book. His input helped us over some tough hurdles.

Above all, we appreciate the confidence shown by the NRECA Board of Directors in authorizing this project when it was hardly more than a gleam in the editor's eyes.

To Bob Partridge, Bob Bergland and our colleagues at NRECA and throughout rural electrification: Thanks for your encouragement, thanks for pitching in when asked, and thanks for giving us elbow room when we needed it.

Public and Association Affairs Department Director Bob Nelson provided valuable guidance and was always ready with support. Special thanks to Phil McMartin for expertly taping and producing video material to help promote the book.

NRECA's members quickly responded to our calls for specific photos, and they ordered—largely on faith—enough copies to make the publication economically feasible.

Heartfelt thanks to McArdle Printing's Ralph Ives, who was both midwife and nursemaid. For Ralph—so many years a part of the "rural electric family" as printer of NRECA publications—this was a "swan song." Even after his retirement in July, he kept a helpful eye on us. Ralph's successor, Bob Smith, picked up the project in midstream and quickly became a welcome addition—and advocate. The craftsmen at McArdle also "adopted" this project and were as watchful for imperfections as the most demanding of us.

Diane Hamilton, a photo researcher with a vast knowledge of the agricultural and rural collections at the Archives and the Library of Congress, discovered many excellent photos.

Erma Angevine's practiced, thoughtful eye as "the final proofer" has, we're sure, minimized our errors.

We appreciate the faith expressed by three former REA Administrators—David Hamil, Norman Clapp and Robert Feragen—by lending their names to promotional material even before the book was into production. We also thank Bob Feragen for allowing us to print his epic poem, "A Celebration of Success." This poem should confirm his place as the "poet laureate" of rural electrification, and we believe it to be a perfect signature to the book.

We are indebted to many others who willingly gave of their time and expertise. Many—we hope all—of these individual and organizational names can be found in the credits section in the back of the book.

My greatest debt, as always, is to my wife, Ellyn, and to my children for their encouragement, support and understanding throughout the many months of this project.

—Richard A. Pence
September, 1984

Table of Contents

1

2

Before Humankind, before the primordial dawn of living things, before an Earth even, there was the mass.

Swirling in the Universe of space and time back billions of years, the mass was a formless and wild fireworks of gaseous dust. There was an energy working within it, setting off a secret chemistry of shaping, of solidifying.

A crust formed. Escaping gases created a moist atmosphere of solid cloud. The mass came to be swamp and forest, glacier and river, desert and mountain, continent and sea. Earth.

This was before the cell and tissue and bone that form living things. Before there was ear to hear the forming and roaring, the clashing and crashing over the geologic ages. Before the eye and the beholding of the eye. Before Humankind and feeling and pain. Before knowing.

Here in the midst of the eons, but an hour ago on geology's clock, there came the living things, first of water, then of the water and the land, slithering across the crust of the planet. Later, footed creatures with hooves, miniature at first, then dinosaurs, then fierce mammoths, crashed across the strange landscape, terrorizing Humankind, which had only just arrived.

Humankind, fearful of the giant creatures of water, land and sky, fearful of the fire and lightning. But curious. Humankind, on a groping journey of discovery, learning of the elements of fire, water, air, the Earth itself, seeking to harness the wild energies, unlock the powerful secrets.

Hands. Humankind had hands to hold and probe. And the curiosity to wonder and seek and dream.

The hands of Thales the Greek rubbed the amber. The amber became a magnet, pulling to itself light objects. ηλεκτρον. The Greek word for amber. Electron. Electricity. Sir William Gilbert called the phenomenon electricity when he issued his great work *De Magnete* in 1600 A.D.

The hands of Otto von Guericke in 1660 created the first light from electricity. One rotated a ball of sulfur with a crank and the other rubbed the ball, producing crackling noises and small flashes of light.

Science—pure and applied—then made steady progress in unlocking electricity's secrets. In the grand design that is always part inquiry, part accident, Humankind's detectives fiddled with frogs' legs, flew kites, advanced postulates, theorems and laws.

By mid-19th century, the Leyden jars, the copper wires and coils, the carbon, sulfur and zinc were set aside. No longer the plaything of dreamers, electricity left the realm of theory and experimentation to become the preoccupation and purview of inventor, planner, engineer. They would capture it, harness it, leverage it and deliver it. It became all-pervasive, omnipresent. It lighted streets and homes, drove the engines of industry, sent signals and voices across the continents and the oceans.

The hands—and mind—of Thomas Alva Edison in 1879 invented an incandescent lamp which burned continuously for two days, then a bulb which would burn for several hundred hours. In 1882 he opened the Pearl Street Station, which generated and delivered power by direct current throughout New York's lower Manhattan district, providing "central station

3

4

service" for street lighting and homes. America and the industrial nations of the West charged into the 20th century on a trip propelled by electricity. By the dawning of the "American Century," lights glowed in every major city and they rapidly reached out to town, village and hamlet. Electricity and the "bright lights," now part of American folklore, were among the powerful forces transforming America from an agrarian to an industrial and urban nation.

But part of the society of Humankind, the rural people of America, was not to know electricity. They were told that, for them, it was not a commercial proposition. There was no profit in it. And because there was no profit, there were no lights for rural people. Sadly, what electricity did for them was to illuminate difference.

Because there was no electric connection, because it was unattainable under the established economic order of the time, a great gulf developed. Two nations, two classes, two centuries: One of light, one of darkness. One "backward," one "enlightened."

Electricity: Provider of power to drive the cities' factories. Electricity: The magical commercial commodity giving off the fascinating glow of "The Great White Way." Electricity: Beckoning millions of the rural young to leave the land. Electricity: The divider.

Temperance leaders, muckraking novelists and moralists allied the "bright lights" to city evils, to corruption of rural sister and son. Yet rural sister and son continued to leave the benighted land. And agricultural endeavor and rural life remained little changed from what it had been decades before.

Hear the rural leaders of the late 19th century as they speak of the chains of their imprisoning drudgery and darkness: "Go into the country and you will find numberless cases of men with poor health, crushed energies, ruined constitutions, and stunted souls, and women the slaves of habits of excess labor. It is not honorable, it is not a trait of true nobility, to bring up children to this thankless, unrequited labor."

Yet the rural people and their organizations that sought justice in their land remained strangely tranquil, hopeful. The "opening song" at the Grange meeting that heard the above fiery words underscores their belief that justice in the land would come through deliverance Divine:

As a mighty host with banners,
Peaceful victories will we gain,
Moved by Right's resistless purpose,
Held by Love's electric chain;
Moved by Right's resistless purpose,
Held by Love's electric chain.

But justice and dignity were not to come to them in such sublime fashion. The "electric chain" *would* be set in motion, by a quiet revolution that stirred the hearts and spirits of the rural people of America.

But not now. For now, the dread cycle of drudgery and despair, the ceaseless, mindless and numbing labor, filling all their days, all their nights, their seasons and their years, continued, unrelieved, across the darkened land.

Because there was no electricity.

Because There Was No Electricity

I had seen first-hand the grim drudgery and grind which had been the common lot of eight generations of American farm women. I had seen the tallow candle in my own home, followed by the coal-oil lamp. I knew what it was to take care of the farm chores by the flickering, undependable light of the lantern in the mud and cold rains of the fall, and the snow and icy winds of winter.

I had seen the cities gradually acquire a night as light as day.

I could close my eyes and recall the innumerable scenes of the harvest and the unending punishing tasks performed by hundreds of thousands of women, growing old prematurely; dying before their time; conscious of the great gap between their lives and the lives of those whom the accident of birth or choice placed in the towns and cities.

Why shouldn't I have been interested in the emancipation of hundreds of thousands of farm women?

—Senator George W. Norris of Nebraska,
Cosponsor of the Rural Electrification Act

1

2

3

4

5

These excerpts on pages 15-36 are from The Years of Lyndon Johnson: The Path to Power, *by Robert A. Caro. Copyright © 1981, 1982 by Robert A. Caro, Inc. Reprinted by permission of the publisher, Alfred A. Knopf, Inc.*

Because there was no electricity, a farmer could not use an electric pump. He was forced not only to milk but to water his cows by hand, a chore that, in dry weather, meant hauling up endless buckets from a deep well. Because he could not use an electric auger, he had to feed his livestock by hand, pitchforking heavy loads of hay up into the loft of his barn and then stomping on it to soften it enough so the cows could eat it. He had to prepare the feed by hand: because he could not use an electric grinder, he would get the corn kernels for his mules and horse by sticking ears of corn—hundreds of ears of corn—one by one into a corn sheller and cranking it for hours. Because he could not use electric motors, he had to unload cotton seed by hand, and then shovel it into the barn by hand; to saw wood by hand, by swinging an axe or riding one end of a ripsaw. Because there was never enough daylight for all the jobs that had to be done, the farmer usually finished after sunset, ending the day as he had begun it, stumbling around the barn milking the cows in the dark, as farmers had done centuries before.

Washing, ironing, cooking, canning, shearing, helping with the plowing and the picking and the sowing, and, every day, carrying the water and wood, and because there was no electricity, having to do everything by hand by the same methods that had been employed by her mother and grandmother and great-great-great-grandmother before her.

. . . hauling the water, hauling the wood, canning, washing, ironing, helping with the shearing, the plowing and picking.

Because there was no electricity.

1

The farmer had to milk his cows by hand—arising at three-thirty or four o'clock in the morning to do so, because milking was a time-consuming chore (more than two hours for twenty cows) and it had to be finished by daylight: every hour of daylight was needed for work in the fields. Milking was done by the dim light of kerosene lanterns. . . . Or it was done in the dark. And there was a constant danger of fire with kerosene lamps, and even a spark could burn down a hay-filled barn, and destroy a farmer's last chance of holding on to his place, so many farmers were afraid to use a lantern in the barn.

Because without electricity there could be no refrigerator, the milk was kept on ice. The ice was expensive and farmers had to lug it from town at enormous cost in time. . . . And often even the ice didn't help. Farmers would have to take the milk out of their pit and place it by the roadside to be picked up by the trucks from [the] dairies, but often the trucks would be late, and the milk would sit outside. . . . Even if it was not actually spoiled, the dairy would refuse to accept it if its temperature was above fifty degrees Fahrenheit—and when the truck driver pulled his thermometer out, a farmer, seeing the red line above fifty, would know that his hours of work in the barn in the dark had been for nothing.

2

3

1

2

3

4

A farmer would try to keep a supply of wood in the house, or, if he had sons old enough, would assign the task to them. They would cut down the trees and chop them into four-foot lengths that could be stacked in cords. When wood was needed in the house, they would cut it into shorter lengths and split the pieces so they could fit into the stoves. But as with the water, these chores often fell to the women.

The necessity of hauling the wood was not, however, the principal reason so many farm wives hated their wood stoves. In part, they hated these stoves because they were so hard to "start up." The damper that opened into the firebox created only a small draft even on a breezy day, and on a windless day, there was no draft—because there was no electricity, of course, there was no fan to move the air in the kitchen—and a fire would flicker out time after time. . . . In part, farm wives hated wood stoves because they were so dirty, because the smoke from the wood blackened walls and ceilings, and ashes were always escaping through the grating, and the ash box had to be emptied twice a day—a dirty job and dirtier if, while the ashes were being carried outside, a gust of wind scattered them around inside the house. They hated the stoves because they could not be left unattended. Without devices to regulate the heat and keep the temperature steady, when the stove was being used for baking or some other cooking in which an even temperature was important, a woman would have to keep a constant watch on the fire, thrusting logs—or corncobs, which ignited quickly—into the firebox every time the heat slackened.

Most of all, they hated them because they were so hot.

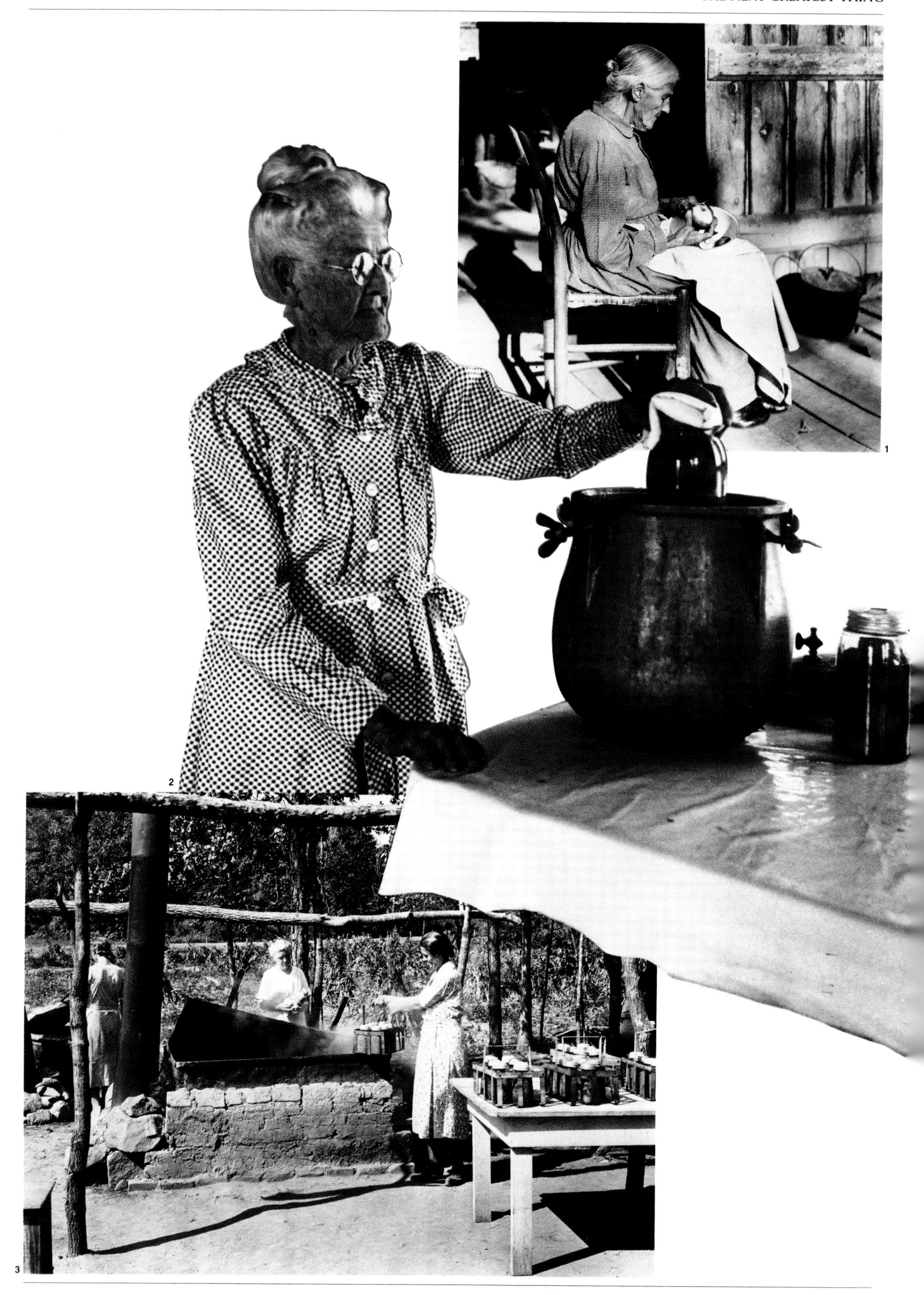

1

2

3

4

5

Since—because there was no electricity—there were no refrigerators, vegetables or fruit had to be canned the very day they came ripe. And, from June through September, something was coming ripe almost every day, it seemed; on a single peach tree, the fruit on different branches would come ripe on different days. In a single orchard, the peaches might be reaching ripeness over a span as long as two weeks. . . . And after the peaches, the strawberries would begin coming ripe, and then the gooseberries, and then the blueberries. The tomatoes would become ripe before the okra, the okra before the zucchini, the zucchini before the corn. So the canning would go on with only brief intervals—all summer.

Canning required constant attendance on the stove. Since boiling water was essential, the fire in the stove had to be kept roaring hot, so logs had to be continually put into the firebox. At least twice during a day's canning, moreover—probably three or four times—a woman would have to empty the ash container, which meant wrestling the heavy, unwieldy device out from under the firebox. And when the housewife wasn't bending down to the flames, she was standing over them. In canning fruit, for example, first sugar was dropped into the huge iron canning pot, and watched carefully and stirred constantly, so that it would not become lumpy, until it was completely dissolved. Then the fruit—perhaps peaches, which would have been

6

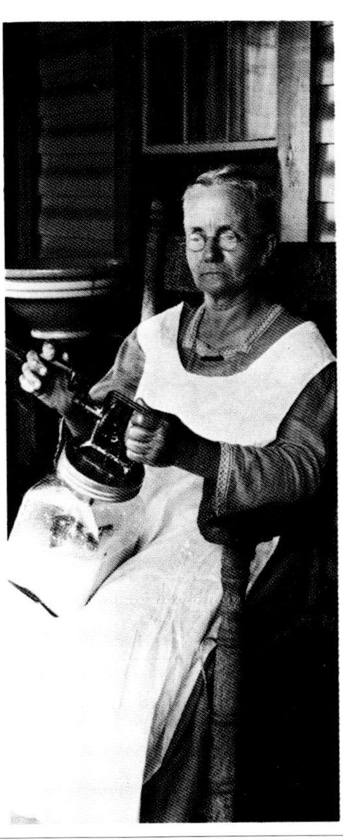
7

8

1

peeled earlier—was put in the pot, and boiled until it turned into a soft and mushy jam that would be packed into jars (which would have been boiling—to sterilize them—in another pot) and sealed with wax. Boiling the peaches would take more than an hour, and during that time they had to be stirred constantly so that they would not stick to the pot. And when one load of peaches was finished, another load would be put in, and another. Canning was an all-day job. So when a woman was canning, she would have to spend all day in a little room with a tin or sheet-iron roof on which a blazing sun was beating down without mercy, standing in front of the iron stove and wood fire within it. And every time the heat in that stove died down even a bit, she would have to make it hotter again.

And there was no respite. If a bunch of peaches came ripe a certain day, that was the day they had to be canned—no matter how the housewife might feel that day. . . . And once the canning process was begun, it could not stop. "If you peeled six dozen peaches, and then, later that day, you felt sick," you couldn't stop, says Gay Harris. "Because you can't can something if it's rotten. The job has to be done the same day, no matter what." Sick or not, when it was time to can, a woman canned, standing hour after hour, trapped between a blazing sun and a blazing wood fire. "We had no choice, you see," Mrs. Harris says.

2

3

4

1

2

3

4 5 6 7

Without electricity, even boiling water was work. Anything requiring the use of water was work. . . . And without electricity to work a pump, there was only one way to obtain water: by hand.

The source of water could be either a stream or a well. If the source was a stream, water had to be carried from it to the house. . . . If the source was a well, it had to be lifted to the surface—a bucket at a time.

A farmer would do as much of this pumping and hauling as possible himself, and try to have his sons do as much of the rest as possible. . . . As soon as a youth got big enough to carry the water buckets (which held about four gallons, or thirty-two pounds, of water apiece), he was assigned the job of filling his mother's wash pots before he left for school or the field. . . . But the water the children carried would be used up long before noon, and the children would be away—at school or in the fields—and most of the hauling of water was, therefore, done by women. . . . Carrying it—after she had wrestled off the heavy wooden lid which kept the rats and squirrels out of the well; after she had cranked the bucket up to the surface (and cranking—lifting thirty pounds fifty feet or more—was very hard for most women even with a pulley; most would pull the rope hand over hand, as if they were climbing it, to get their body weight into the effort; they couldn't do it with their arms alone). Says Mrs. Brian Smith of Blanco: "Yes, we had running water. I always said we had running water because I grabbed those two buckets up and ran the two hundred yards to the house with them." But the joking fades away as the memories sharpen. A stooped and bent Hill Country farm wife says, "You see how round-shouldered I am? Well, that's from hauling the water." And, she will often add, "I was round-shouldered like this well before my time, when I was still a young woman. My back got bent from hauling the water, and it got bent when I was still young."

1
2
3
4

5

Every week, every week all year long—every week without fail—there was washday.

The wash was done outside. A huge vat of boiling water would be suspended over a larger, roaring fire and near it three large "Number Three" zinc washtubs and a dishpan would be placed on a bench.

The clothes would be scrubbed in the first of the zinc tubs, scrubbed on a washboard by a woman bending over the tub. The soap, since she couldn't afford store-bought soap, was soap she had made from lye, soap that was not very effective, and the water was hard. Getting farm dirt out of clothes required hard scrubbing.

Then the farm wife would wring out each piece of clothing to remove from it as much as possible of the dirty water, and put it in the big vat of boiling water. Since the scrubbing would not have removed all of the dirt, she would try to get the rest out by "punching" the clothes in the vat—standing over the boiling water and using a wooden paddle or, more often, a broomstick, to stir the clothes and swish them through the water and press them against the bottom or sides, moving the broom handle up and down and around as hard as she could for ten or fifteen minutes in a human imitation of the agitator of an automatic—electric—washing machine.

The next step was to transfer the clothes from the boiling water to the second of the three zinc washtubs: The "rinse tub." The clothes were lifted out of the big vat on the end of the broomstick, and held up on the end of the stick for a few minutes while the dirty water dripped out.

When the clothes were in the rinse tub, the woman bent over the tub and rinsed them, by swishing each individual item through the water. Then she wrung out the clothes, to get as

1

2

3

4

much of the dirty water out as possible, and placed the clothes in the third tub, which contained bluing, and swished them around in *it*—this time to get the bluing all through the garment and make it white—and then repeated the same movements in the dishpan, which was filled with starch.

At this point, one load of wash would be done.

For each load, the water in each of the three washtubs would have to be changed. A washtub held about eight gallons. Since the water had to be warm, the woman would fill each tub half with boiling water from the big pot and half with cold water. She did the filling with a bucket which held three or four gallons—twenty-five or thirty pounds. For the first load or two of wash, the water would have been provided by her husband or her sons. But after this water had been used up, part of washday was walking—over and over—that long walk to the spring or well, hauling up the water, hand over laborious hand, and carrying those heavy buckets back. Another part of washday was also a physical effort: the "punching" of the clothes in the big vat. . . . Lifting the clothes out of the vat was an effort, too. A dripping mass of soggy clothes was heavy, and it felt heavier when it had to be lifted out of that vat and held up for minutes at a time so that the dirty water could drip out, and then swung over the rinsing tub. . . . Even the wringing was, after a few hours, an effort. . . . And her hands—from scrubbing with lye soap and wringing—were raw and swollen. Of course, there was also the bending—hours of bending—over the rub boards. . . . Hauling the water, scrubbing, punching, rinsing: a farm wife did this for hours on end—while a city wife did it by pressing the button on her electric washing machine.

5

6

1

2

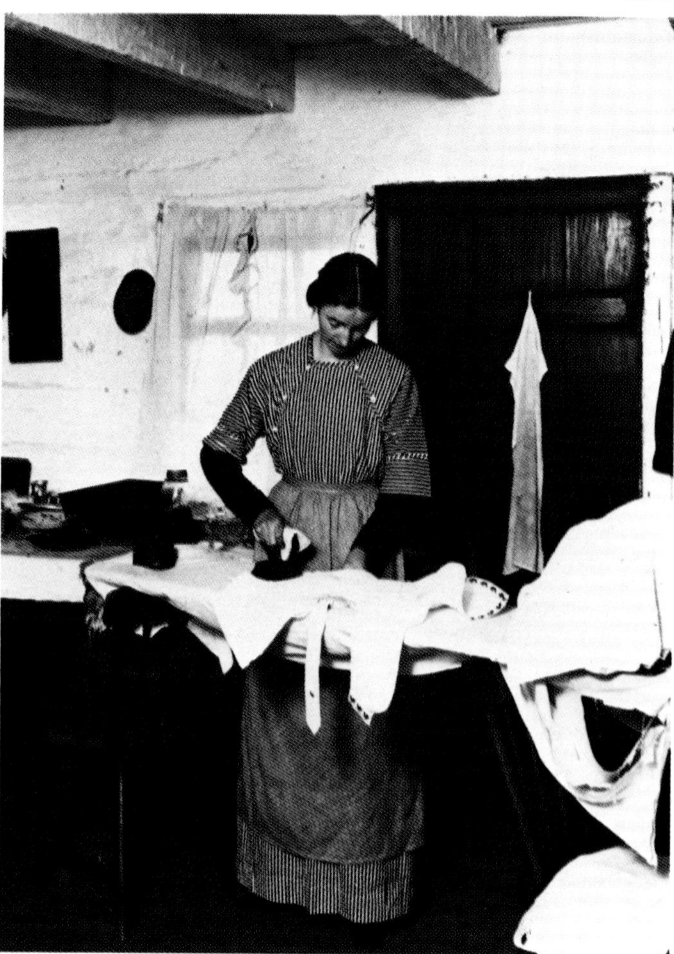

3

4

Washday was Monday. Tuesday was for ironing.

The Department of Agriculture finds that "Young women today are not aware of the origin of the word 'iron,' as they press clothes with lightweight appliances of aluminum or hollow stainless steel." In the 1930s an iron was an *iron*—a six- or seven-pound wedge of iron. The irons used had to be heated on the wood stove, and they would retain their heat for only a few minutes—a man's shirt generally required two irons; a farm wife would own three or four of them, so that several could be heating while one was working.

Since burning wood generates soot, the irons became dirty as they sat heating on the stove. Or, if any moisture was left on an iron from the sprinkled clothes on which it had just been used, even the thinnest smoke from the stove created a muddy film on the bottom. The irons had to be cleaned frequently, therefore, by scrubbing them with a rag that had been dipped in salt, and if the soot was too thick, they had to be sanded and scraped. And no matter how carefully you checked the bottom of the irons, and sanded and scraped them, there would often remain some little spot of soot—as you would discover when you rubbed it over a clean white shirt or dress. Then you had to wash that item of clothing over again.

The irons would burn a woman's hand. The wooden handle or the potholder would slip, and she would have searing metal against her flesh; by noon, she might have blister atop blister—on hands that had to handle the rag that had been dipped in salt. . . . But again the worst aspect of ironing was the heat. On ironing day, a fire would have to be blazing in the wood stove all day, filling the kitchen, hour after hour, with heat and smoke.

1

2

3

4

So many conveniences taken for granted in American cities were unknown . . . not just vacuum cleaners and washing machines but, for example, bathrooms, since, as a practical matter, indoor plumbing is unfeasible without running water, which requires an electric pump. In the summer, bathing could be done in the creek (when the creek wasn't dry); in the winter, it entailed lugging in water and heating it on the stove (which entailed lugging in wood) before pouring it into a Number Three washtub.

5

1

2

3

4

The circle of light cast by a kerosene lamp was small, and there were seldom enough lamps in the home of an impoverished farm family. If a family had so many children that they completely surrounded the one good lamp while studying, their mother could not do her sewing until they were finished. And outside the small circles of light, the rooms of a farmhouse were dark.

Evening was often the only time in which farm couples could read, but the only light for reading came from kerosene lamps. In movies about the Old West, these lamps appear so homy that it is difficult for a city dweller to appreciate how much—and why—some farm dwellers disliked them so passionately.

5

1

Lighting the kerosene lamp was a frustrating job. . . . Keeping it lit was even more frustrating. It burned straight across for only a moment, and then would either flare up or die down to an inadequate level. Even when the wick was trimmed just right, a kerosene lamp provided only limited illumination. The approximately twenty-five watts of light provided by most such lamps was adequate for children doing their homework—although surveys would later find that the educational level of rural children improved markedly immediately upon the introduction of electricity—but their parents, whose eyes were not so strong, had more difficulty. . . . Pointing to deep vertical lines between her eyebrows, more than one farm wife says: "So many of us have these lines from squinting to read."

2

3

4

Finding the Way

The seeds of the rural electric dream were sown in the early years of the 20th century. During this fertile time of progressive public reform and political ferment, the dream of rural power germinated among wider visions and struggles of the era:

POPULISM: Conscience and soul of rural outrage, discontent.

PROGRESSIVISM: Tamer and moderator of private greed, public neglect.

CONSERVATION: Steward and servant of nature and humankind.

COOPERATION: Leaven and lever of human enterprise.

These were the main elements of turn-of-the-century thought fusing in the idea of rural electrification.

Chief among these forerunning elements was the American conservation movement and its underlying principle: "The greatest good for the greatest number for the longest time." Carrying this principle forward was the concept of federal multiple-use development of river systems for flood control, water supply, irrigation, *electric power,* and recreation.

President Theodore Roosevelt, "godfather" of the American conservation movement, put his power and persuasion behind its ideas and ideals. His chief forester, the aristocratic Gifford Pinchot, was its "prophet" and visionary. This movement set down early 20th century lines of thought that led to the successful electrification of rural America. Opposite page: Pinchot relating a tall story to the President as they steam upon the Mississippi River during a 1907 meeting of the Inland Waterways Commission.

Theodore Roosevelt articulated the grand design: *"Each river system, from its headwaters in the forest to its mouth, a single unit"*—to be used consistently and coherently for the benefit of the people.

To protect the public interest there was established as early as 1906—by law—the "preference principle," which assured that the benefits of the power from federal projects would flow to the people rather than the private interests. The availability of this federal power for public purposes would serve as a "yardstick" of the cost of producing and delivering electricity.

Roosevelt firmly planted the "yardstick" principle in federal policy by vetoing, on three separate occasions, bills which would have granted unrestricted private hydroelectric power development.

He and his chief forester, Gifford Pinchot, understood well the need for federal protection of the nation's natural resources. But Roosevelt, as "godfather" of the American conservation movement, and Pinchot, as its "prophet," also foresaw, though in shadowy outline, the enormous human benefits and potentials to be derived. In their vision were sown the dreams of the rural power that succeeding generations of leaders and thinkers would pursue.

The way to fulfillment would be arduous and marked by many changes of fortune. But the dreams, though deferred, endured through a remarkable quest, peopled with a rich pageantry of players. . . .

1

TR: 'Farmers Above All Should Have That Power'

It is the obvious duty of the Government to call the attention of farmers to the growing monopolization of water power. The farmers above all should have that power, on reasonable terms, for cheap transportation, for lighting their homes, and for innumerable uses in the daily tasks on the farm.

—President Theodore Roosevelt,
Message of Transmittal to Congress,
Report of the Country Life Commission,
February 9, 1909

The early populists, progressives and conservationists—grass rooters in tandem with Ivy League reformers—were appalled at the circumstances under which rural Americans lived and worked. They saw the drudgery-ridden rural conditions as a national disgrace. There was alarm at the hundreds of thousands of rural young leaving for the cities. Rural America was becoming the primitive backwash of a society undergoing rapid industrialization and urbanization. This social concern, allied with the conservation ethic, was reflected by the work of the Country Life Commission, a fact-finding board appointed by President Theodore Roosevelt, at the suggestion of Gifford Pinchot, to call attention to the increasing disparities between rural and city life.

The Country Life Commission Report of 1909 was a compassionate document which brought to public light the incredible lack of services and conveniences in rural areas which had for years been considered as necessities in the cities. The report was particularly critical of the lot of the rural woman: "The burden of the hardships falls most heavily on the farmer's wife than on the farmer himself. Her life is the more monotonous and the more isolated, no matter what the wealth or poverty of the family may be. . . ."

In its lengthy conclusions the commission made pointed references to the lack of electric power and light on farms, and recommended ways rural people might possibly obtain them, either through use of federal hydroelectric power or by organizing cooperatives. It was the first, official expression of federal concern over the need to electrify the rural areas.

The introduction of effective agricultural cooperation throughout the United States is of first importance. . . . Organized associative effort (cooperatives) may take on special forms. . . . It may have for its object the securing of telephone service, the extension of electric lines, the improvement of highways, and other forms of betterment.

—Report of the Country Life Commission,
February 9, 1909

2

Chairman Bailey noted that state agricultural colleges, experiment stations and the U.S. Department of Agriculture had a great store of knowledge, but the fundamental farm problem remained: "How can the farmer and his family realize the best home life, the best business life and the best social life on the farm?"

3

Commission Chairman Liberty Hyde Bailey, Dean of the School of Agriculture at Cornell University, stated: "The country life movement is the working out of the desire to make rural civilization as effective and satisfying as other civilizations. . . . It is a world motive to even-up society as between country and city."

4

Chief forester Gifford Pinchot served on the commission and had first suggested the idea of it. "My work in forestry had brought me into contact with life on the farm in many parts of the U.S. I had seen no little of its hardships, and especially of the hardships of women, and I was more than glad to help."

5

"Uncle" Henry Wallace, editor of Wallace's Farmer, *and father and grandfather of two "Henrys" who would later become U.S. Secretaries of Agriculture, was an influential and diligent member of the commission. Wallace actively promoted the recommendations of the commission in his farm journal.*

6

Sir Horace Plunkett, a settler on the Montana frontier, contributed expertise he had gained from Ireland's agricultural co-op movement. The Country Life Commission advocated that farmers use cooperatives to organize and obtain services and realize economic and social goals.

'I Am a Public Engineer and Not a Private Engineer'

—*Morris Llewellyn Cooke, 1920*

As America moved into the second decade of the 20th century, the progressive public works of Theodore Roosevelt and his conservationists left a continuing agenda for a future generation of leaders.

Here was a new breed. Schooled in the professions, in science, technology and the law, this second generation of activist-thinkers believed that the benefits of science and technology could be fused to achieve a higher level of public good and bring about a better and more humane society.

One adherent to the progressive ideal was the eminent Philadelphia engineer, Morris Llewellyn Cooke. As director of Philadelphia's public works department from 1911 to 1915, during the term of reform-minded Mayor Rudolph Blankenburg, Cooke took the 4,000 city works' employees out of local politics, placing them on civil service rolls. He gained for the city's electric rate-payers and citizens a million-dollar annual electric rate reduction and a cash rebate of $180,000 through an unprecedented and victorious battle in the courts against the excessive and unfair practices of the Philadelphia Electric Company.

Cooke had railed against the unwillingness of the utility industry to translate new technologies into economic and social progress for powerless rural families. The exodus of the rural people continued unabated—in the millions. He saw this exodus as a diseased social condition with severe implications for national stability—and he envisioned rural electrification as a means to help stem this tide.

Public leaders, concerned with the alarming out-migration of rural people and the wretched conditions of those left behind, sought out the expertise and commitment of Cooke to begin electrifying rural America. One of these was Gifford Pinchot, the newly elected governor of Pennsylvania.

Pinchot commissioned Cooke in 1923 to conduct a "Giant Power" survey of the state to study electric potential for the future of industry, railroads, homes—and farms—in the com-

Many of the reforms promised by Philadelphia Mayor Rudolph ("Old Dutch Cleanser") Blankenburg (center, breaking ground for the Philadelphia parkway) were fulfilled by his public-spirited and able Director of Public Works Morris L. Cooke (at Blankenburg's right hand in bowler hat), who initiated many "clean-up" actions against patronage and corruption.

monwealth. Cooke sent out a call to engineers and lawyers who had worked with him on the earlier Philadelphia Electric case, assembling an impressive team of progressive professionals—"socially minded" engineers.

The team developed a broad-scale energy development plan with rural electrification playing a big part of it. Abundant supplies of power generated from plants close to the Pennsylvania coal fields would be shipped over giant transmission lines. The power would be moved to all power distributors and made available from a statewide pool. Farmers' power costs would be driven down by widespread use and rural electric rates would decline. They would be able to serve themselves through local public ownership districts or through new distributing corporations—co-ops.

But the Giant Power concepts were too bold and innovative for the conservative climate of the times and the Pennsylvania Legislature would not provide the broad authorities necessary for the plan.

2

Governor Pinchot called for a far-sighted and ambitious Giant Power plan in Pennsylvania that would electrify the commonwealth's rural areas. The Pennsylvania Legislature of 1925-1926 would have none of it.

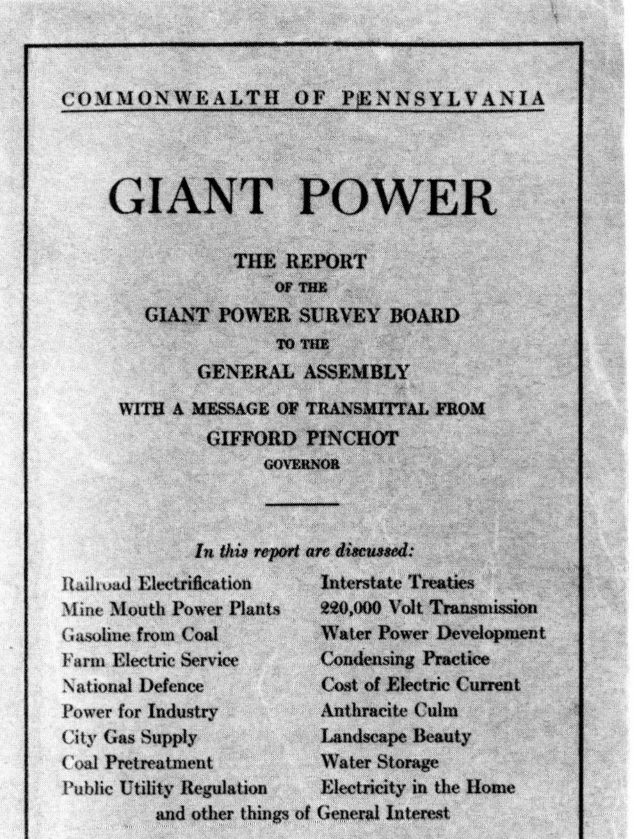

COMMONWEALTH OF PENNSYLVANIA

GIANT POWER

THE REPORT
OF THE
GIANT POWER SURVEY BOARD
TO THE
GENERAL ASSEMBLY
WITH A MESSAGE OF TRANSMITTAL FROM
GIFFORD PINCHOT
GOVERNOR

In this report are discussed:

Railroad Electrification	Interstate Treaties
Mine Mouth Power Plants	220,000 Volt Transmission
Gasoline from Coal	Water Power Development
Farm Electric Service	Condensing Practice
National Defence	Cost of Electric Current
Power for Industry	Anthracite Culm
City Gas Supply	Landscape Beauty
Coal Pretreatment	Water Storage
Public Utility Regulation	Electricity in the Home

and other things of General Interest

Issued at the Capitol at Harrisburg, February 1925

3

Otto M. Rau 4

George H. Morse 5

The progressive Giant Power plan to electrify rural Pennsylvania would have a profound influence in ultimately piercing economic and technical barriers to rural electrification. In addition to Cooke, who headed the study, the principal members of the team were pioneering electrical engineer Otto M. Rau, rural electrification specialist George H. Morse, and Judson C. Dickerman, assistant director. Morse and Dickerman had worked with Cooke on the Philadelphia Electric Co. rate case.

Judson C. Dickerman 6

Above: The members of the Power Authority of the State of New York were appointed by Governor Roosevelt in May, 1931. In June the trustees began work and posed with the governor. From left, Morris Llewellyn Cooke, Delos M. Cosgrove, Herbert H. Lehman, Frank R. Walsh, chairman; Roosevelt, Fred J. Freestone, and James C. Bonbright. Below: The newly elected Governor Roosevelt dictates answers to telegrams at his Warm Springs cottage with his personal secretary Mr. V. Warwick Halsey.

'Giant Power,' Revisited

The Giant Power study, although defeated in Pennsylvania, gained attention nationwide. It was circulated widely and became a guide for investigations of rural electrification in several states. It caught the attention of the new governor of New York—another of the controversial Roosevelts—Franklin Delano.

The prestige won by Cooke through the Pennsylvania survey made him a logical choice to serve as a consulting member of the Power Authority of the State of New York (PASNY) when Roosevelt created it in 1931 to look into development of power from the St. Lawrence River by the United States and Canada.

One of Cooke's responsibilities as a member of PASNY was to develop information about distribution costs to plan for power marketing to farmers and small consumers.

Now there was a working laboratory. Many of the specialists and engineers on the New York project were carry-overs from Cooke's Giant Power days—notably Otto M. Rau and Judson C. Dickerman. Making use of their earlier knowledge and research, they cut through the maze of utility cost accounting figures.

In a rare pre-presidential glimpse of the fighting polio victim, New York Governor Franklin D. Roosevelt chatting on a park bench with Pennsylvania Governor Gifford Pinchot at a 1931 Governors' meeting in French Lick, Indiana. Below: Roosevelt grew determined to find a way to bring economical electricity to farmers after he got his power bill for his rural cottage in Georgia in 1924. The rate, 18 cents a kilowatt-hour, "was about four times what I paid at Hyde Park, New York. That started my long study of public utility charges for electric current and the whole subject of getting electricity in farm homes," he later related. "So it can be said that a little cottage at Warm Springs, Georgia, was the birthplace of the Rural Electrification Administration."

3

4

The study team, finding that 24-hour operating conditions of power plants made cost recoveries drastically lower, successfully attacked the proposition that a mile of line in a rural area cost nearly $2,000. They analyzed all the elements that went into building a power line—poles, transformers, wire, labor, the costs of engineers and engineering firms, the cost of management—all overhead charges. They determined that a mile of rural line would be $300 to $1,500 cheaper than the power companies claimed.

Now, said Cooke, "Widespread rural electrification is socially and economically desirable and financially both sound and feasible."

The utility companies did not hail the findings as the signal to proceed full tilt towards electrifying the countryside. And this time it truly was not economically feasible for them to undertake it. For the country was moving steadily deeper into the greatest economic depression it had ever experienced.

As it turned out, the Great Depression itself—and how and who the American people chose to challenge it—had everything to do with the "do-ability" and future of rural electrification.

1

ALLIANCE OF DESPAIR: Drought, Dust, Depression

When the Great Depression swept across all of America with devastating force in the early 1930s, rural America had known and suffered its effects—the wrenching heartbreak and dislocation—for nearly a decade. The droughts, poor harvests and low farm prices of the 1920s had made the countryside the spawning ground and harbinger of the general despair that took hold of an entire nation. The Great Depression was "farm-led and farm-fed," rural people reminded their city cousins, who were just then learning of the hard times the people on the land had experienced for years. Many farm families left the land forever. They just gave up and got out. Even during the relatively good farming years of the first two decades of the 20th century, few of the rural people had been able to obtain "the electric." Now, it seemed, it would never be.

2

3

1

In the middle of that night the wind passed on and left the land quiet. The dust-filled air muffled sound more completely than fog does. The people, lying in their beds, heard the wind stop. . . . In the morning the dust hung like fog, and the sun was as red as ripe new blood. All day the dust sifted down from the sky, and the next day it sifted down. An even blanket covered the earth. It settled on the corn, piled up on the tops of the fence posts, piled up on the wires; it settled on roofs, blanketed the weeds and trees.

—*John Steinbeck, from* The Grapes of Wrath

2

3 4

5

1

Vegetation does not grow, streams have run dry. Springs have failed. Trees, with leaves blighted, provide little or no shade. Cattle, lacking proper moisture, cannot put on flesh. Soil, turned to dust, drifts over the once-fertile grazing lands. The sun pours down unbelievable heat. The weather observer in Topeka, Kansas, stated today that only twice in 27 days has the temperature failed to reach 98 degrees; only four times has it fallen below 70 degrees at night. . . . For the last week the average daily maximum temperature has been 107 degrees. Temperatures . . . in some communities have been 114 degrees often, sometimes as high as 117. . . . The produce truck has been replaced on the highways by the water wagon. . . . Near Oklahoma City today 600 head of cattle have been shot after a futile search for water . . . hundreds of others were to be destroyed . . . sharecropping farmers in Oklahoma were deserting their homes . . . stores are doing a poor business, and schools are wholly or partially closed.

—*New York Times report, circa 1935*

2

3

4

1

2

They called it the Farmers' Holiday Association—the "Holiday" in it intended ironically to underscore the economic distress of the time: The banks were in the habit of declaring "holidays" as they went "bust" and closed their doors, sometimes to recoup, sometimes forever.

Now it was the farmers' turn. Faced with the loss of everything they owned, many followed the lead of the Iowa Farmers Union and its leader, Milo Reno, in their efforts to withhold farm products and force prices up. Their ditty went:

Let's call a "Farmers' Holiday,"
A Holiday let's hold.
We'll eat our wheat and ham and eggs,
And let them eat their gold.

Burleigh County

FARMERS - WORKERS

Mass - Meeting

CITY AUDITORIUM

Bismarck, Saturday, August 1st., 1:00 P.M.

Our economic struggle has become unbearable, due to the condition of drought. Starvation of humans as well as animals is facing us all.

Something must be done immediately to save mankind and beasts from real suffering.

This Burleigh County Mass Meeting has been called by The Burleigh County Holiday Association, supported by The American Federation of Labor, The North Dakota Labor Association, Inc., The State Unification Committee of WPA Workers, The Workers Labor Club of Bismarck.

This distress and condition for food is the people's question, and must be discussed by the people. For this purpose this mass meeting has been called. This is your meeting, you are expected to be present with all your friends and neighbors.

TOPICS TO BE DISCUSSED

1. The immediate relief of food for man and beast.
2. An American living wage scale for all workers on projects.
3. Pension for all old age people.
4. Winter consideration, such as coal, shelter, clothing, food for humans as well as animals.
5. How can such mass meetings spread into every county of this state, and into every state of this nation?
6. Unification of all Farm Organizations and Labor Organizations, upon the question of The Right to Live, food, clothing, and shelter.
7. Any other, non-political, question which concerns the farmer and the worker at this time.

Burleigh County Holiday Association, Fred Argast, President
American Federation of Labor, Adam Voight, Chairman Bismarck Central Labor Body
Burleigh County Labor Association, Frank Walker, President
Workers Labor Club of Bismarck, Gene Hunt, President

3

4

1

2

Pioneer strength was not always enough to make farming a success. The faces of the settlers showed the worry and hardships. After the few good years during the first two decades of the 20th century, there came drought and serious decreases in farm prices. Finally, the Great Depression brought a crushing blow to the entire nation. With the drought and dust storms, the effects were devastating. Bankers foreclosed mortgages; entire families drifted to the cities or the west coast to work as migrant labor. They had lost their homes.

—*Robert W. Feragen,*
from the documentary filmscript,
The Prairie Is Our Garden

3

4

'I Pledge You—I Pledge Myself to a New Deal for the American People.' *—FDR, July, 1932*

March 4, 1933. Inauguration Day for Franklin Delano Roosevelt. All through the night before, urgent calls had been coming in to the President-elect and to outgoing President Herbert Hoover. Governors in dozens of states were ordering bank doors closed to halt withdrawals of currency and gold by desperate, fearful citizens—massive outflows in the hundreds of millions of dollars. Bank holidays declared. The day dawned gray and bleak. In the morning chill, a crowd began forming in front of the Capitol that would swell to more than 100,000 people by noon. A hopeful, fearful nation awaited the new leader's first official words on how he would live up to his pledge of a "New Deal":

Let me first assert my firm belief that the only thing we have to fear is fear itself—nameless, unreasoning, unjustified terror which paralyzes needed efforts to convert retreat into advance.

Those words would be remembered always, but on that day, the words stirring the crowd and the millions riveted to their radios were: "This nation asks for action, and action now. Our greatest primary task is to put people to work. I shall ask the Congress for the one remaining instrument to meet the crisis—broad executive power to wage a war against the emergency, as great as the power that would be given me if we were in fact invaded by a foreign foe."

Always on the mark, humorist Will Rogers described well the public mood of that desperate but hopeful hour, as he wrote: "If he (Roosevelt) burned down the Capitol, we would cheer and say, 'Well, we at least got a fire started somehow.' "

1

Left: Sometimes the New Deal and new jobs meant a new town.

Opposite page, top: Chief Justice of the United States Charles Evans Hughes issuing the oath of office to the new President.

Opposite page, bottom: It was a glum Hoover, worn from the cares of the office, and a confident, ebullient Roosevelt who rode together down Pennsylvania Avenue on Inauguration Day.

2

3

1

President Roosevelt signed the Tennessee Valley Authority (TVA) Act on May 18, 1933—69 days into the legendary "First Hundred Days." In addition to power development, TVA entered into "the wide fields of flood control, soil conservation, reforestation, elimination from agricultural use of marginal lands, and distribution and diversification of industry." The TVA Act was sponsored in the Senate by Sen. George W. Norris of Nebraska (at far right).

2

3

The nation's young men were among the most eager to go to work on the new federal projects. More than 2.5 million of them donned the uniform of the Civilian Conservation Corps (CCC) to work on reforestation, conservation and soil erosion projects in every state. These 1934 "before and after" shots of CCC recruits show what a difference five months—and a haircut, comb, and tie—could make.

4

Translated from legislative and public policy to the language of the local people, TVA and its coming, with its multiple projects to improve a worn-out region, meant jobs. This photograph was taken on November 8, 1933, in Stiner's Store in Lead Mine Bend, Tennessee.

Breathtaking 'First Hundred Days': A Foreshadowing

The New Deal initiatives for economic recovery FDR set in motion in the now-fabled "First Hundred Days" were breathtaking in magnitude and scope.

Wrote columnist Walter Lippmann, "In one week, the nation, which had lost confidence, in everything and everybody, has regained confidence in the government and itself."

Some New Deal ideas and notions would fail, others would be rejected. But in those first hundred days—from March 9 when the Emergency Banking Act was passed, to the enactment of the National Industrial Recovery Act of June 16, 1933—Roosevelt took the country off the gold standard, sent 15 messages to Congress, held a dozen press conferences and introduced and secured passage of 13 pieces of major legislation.

Included were the creation of the Civilian Conservation Corps (CCC), the Agricultural Adjustment Administration (AAA), and the Tennessee Valley Authority (TVA).

The TVA Act, the most enduring achievement of the first hundred days, provided for comprehensive development of the Tennessee River Basin, a desperately poor rural region of washed-out and worn-out soils and souls.

TVA became the highest expression of the single-river system/multiple-use concept of the early Theodore Roosevelt and Gifford Pinchot conservationists. Its dams and reservoirs, among other things, controlled floods, provided navigation and, of course, electric power.

Further, the act provided that "preference" in the sale of power would be given to "States, counties, municipalities and *cooperative organizations of citizens or farmers, not organized or doing business for profit, but primarily for the purpose of supplying electricity to its own citizens or members.*"

That clause was a significant forerunning development that would aid Morris L. Cooke in his advocacy of rural electrification.

Roosevelt had not forgotten Cooke's work in the New York State public power and rural electrification projects, and by late 1933, had cajoled him into joining his Administration. He was named to head the Mississippi Valley Committee, set up to recommend ways to halt the vicious cycle of flood and drought in that vast region.

Cooke had already urged Roosevelt to start a national rural electrification program, but that project was put aside for more pressing needs.

He continued to push, however. In the report of the Mississippi Valley Committee, issued in October, 1934, he stated the case for rural electrification: "Of the returns in terms of social well-being, national safety, agricultural and industrial advance, and of individual happiness and security, there is no yardstick adequate for the measuring."

As Chairman of the Mississippi Valley Committee of the Public Works Administration, Morris L. Cooke (far right, standing) also served as a member of President Roosevelt's National Power Policy Committee. Members of the committee included Interior Secretary Harold L. Ickes (seated, left) and TVA Director David Lilienthal (standing, with Cooke). Other members in the photo, taken at the July, 1934, organizing meeting, are unidentified.

Cooke Makes His Play

After Morris Cooke came to Washington in 1933, he continued his push for a program of rural electrification. But it would have to wait. There were too many New Deal brainstorms and projects clamoring for Roosevelt's attention. Over the months, however, Cooke cultivated formidable allies for the cause. Principal among them was Secretary of the Interior Harold L. Ickes. Eventually he received the green light from Ickes to prepare a proposal. The result was Cooke's now-famous "12-minute memo," a short and remarkably lucid document that successfully made the case for a national plan for rural electrification. Adding to its appeal were flamboyant water-color illustrations showing lots of brilliant red barns (Ickes liked red barns) and a dramatic, black-and-white, zebra-striped cover—designed as an attention-getter amid the sea of Washington paperwork.

Upper left: Morris L. Cooke portrait taken during his REA days. Lower left: Cooke's handwritten introduction to his rural electrification plan. Lower right: Cooke's editorial corrections on a late draft of the "12-minute memo." Opposite: Cooke's "Plan for a Nation-Wide Development of Rural Electrification."

Why rural electrification important

WHAT IS THE TASK

Of the six million farms in the United States over 800,000 are "electrified". But only about 650,000 have "high line" service. The balance have individual Delco plants expensive to operate and limited as to use.

Over 5,000,000 farms are entirely without electric service. Estimates as to the number of these which can now economically be given service range from one to three million.

Unless the Federal government, assisted in particular instances by State and local agencies, assumes an active leadership and complete control only a negligible part of this task can be accomplished. Except in sporadic instances, such as where power is a by-product of an irrigation or flood control project, rural electrification is now the responsibility solely of the private electric interests.

Electrical systems are developed by attaching new construction to that already existant, in large measure because of technical considerations. But it is done also for political advantage to secure exclusive control

- 10 -

'This Report Can Be Read In 12 Minutes'

WHY RURAL ELECTRIFICATION IMPORTANT

Agriculture is a major problem. It must evolve toward the status of a dignified and self-sustaining sector of our social life. So agriculture demands all the *pertinent* production and comfort facilities now available to industry. It must not be conceived, as heretofore, a marginal sector of life. Food and material industries are basic and entitled to corresponding consideration.

Emergence from depression compels a program of public works—i.e. of collective assistance to works having public service character. Those should be favored which (1) contribute to social life, (2) require united investment beyond interest and capacity of private industry. Rural electrification inherently meets these specifications and technically demands large-scale development instead of endless piecemeal extensions.

The reflex influence of widespread rural electrification on the industry providing electric power and light would be enormous. The addition of a small increment of rural extensions has no measurable influence; but large-scale additions of this character would have large measurable and favorable influence on volume, load and demand factors, and on cost per unit of capital investment. The influence on the general rate level and on regulation would be enormous. This development would probably afford the beginnings of real control of the electric industry.

WHAT IS THE TASK?

Of the six million farms in the United States over 800,000 are "electrified." But only about 650,000 have "high line" service. The balance have individual Delco plants, expensive to operate and limited as to use. Over 5,000,000 farms are entirely without electric service. Estimates as to the number of these which can now economically be given service range from one to three million.

Unless the Federal government, assisted in particular instances by State and local agencies, assumes an active leadership and complete control only a negligible part of this task can be accomplished. Except in sporadic instances, such as where power is a by-product of an irrigation or flood control project, rural electrification is now the responsibility solely of the private interests.

Electrical systems are developed by attaching new construction to that already existent, in large measure because of technical considerations. But it is done also for political advantage—to secure exclusive control of a given territory. So strong is this urge for continuity—for having all of a company's territory and lines tied into an integrated system—that in Pennsylvania to connect widely separated areas under common ownership there are strips of chartered territory 200 feet wide where for mile after mile transmission lines are carried without the right of the owner to take off current. Discontinuity or division of the property into isolated segments is taboo within any given system. Hence no private company is likely to create a new center of power production simply in order to serve a rural area.

EXISTING RURAL SERVICE CONSTITUTES THE FRINGE OF THE PRESENT SYSTEM

One reason why only about 10 per cent of the nation's farms are electrified is that at present electric power is largely generated in central stations usually at considerable distance from farming areas. The greater this distance the greater the investment needed to reach the rural consumer and the greater are the energy losses en route. These expenditures in farming areas are relatively less profitable unless rural rates are made high enough. Unlike the railroads or manufacturers the utilities usually require farmers to advance a portion, or all, of the extra investment. Sometimes it is paid in monthly installments over a period of years. . . .

In many cases farm areas can be supplied more economically by small local stations (operated by Diesel oil engine, by water power or even by coal or lignite burning stations—if there is a mine nearby) as the lower cost of generation in the large station may easily be over-balanced by the smaller investment. . . .

The essential elements of a rural electric system are simple and easily manipulated. Distribution involves only poles, wires, transformers and meters. Even the generating units now obtainable require a minimum of attention and are all but fool proof. In Ireland, Norway, New Zealand, Bavaria, Ontario, Switzerland, Alsace and elsewhere a very large part of the rural population have the benefit of electric service.

ADVANTAGES OF RURAL ELECTRIFICATION

Both for the farmer and his wife the introduction of electricity goes a long way toward the elimination of drudgery. The electric refrigerator will effect a considerable change in diet—more fresh vegetables and less salt and cured meats. The inside bathroom, made possible by automatic electric pumping, brings to the farm one of the major comforts of urban life. Electricity will be a strong lever in keeping the boys and girls on the farm—in encouraging reading and other social and cultural activities. As we go into "part-time agriculture" the demand for rural electrification will probably become more insistent.

"The possibility of diversifying our industrial life by sending a fair proportion of it into the rural districts is one of the definite possibilities of the future. Cheap electric power, good roads and automobiles make such a rural industrial development possible." (Address by President Roosevelt at French Lick, Indiana, June, 1931)

Looking even further ahead, widely distributed electricity will become a requisite in the anti-erosion campaign. The tendency must be to discourage corn and cotton and other crops requiring constant harrowing and disturbance of the surface soil, especially in sections having heavy downpours in contrast to a well distributed rainfall. In such regions we must encourage a sod agriculture—meadow land, alfalfa and other legumes—and this means electricity for *moderate* irrigation, for dairying and even for artificially curing grass otherwise uncurable in such climates. . . .

HOW MAKE THE START

Having recognized the advantages of rural electric service and reached the conclusion that only under Governmental leadership and control is any considerable electrification of "dirt farms" possible, the obvious obligation is to get it done. Perhaps the start should be through an allotment of $25,000 or $50,000 to make a survey. But an allotment of $100,000,000 actually to build independent self-liquidating rural projects would exert a mighty influence. . . .

This proposal does not involve competition with private interests as in the case where municipal plants are financed. *This plan calls for entering territory not now occupied* and not likely to be occupied to any considerable extent by private interests. The proposal has only become possible recently through the marvelous development of the Diesel engine.

SOURCE OF POWER FOR RURAL SERVICES

In the public development as here outlined, whether (a) to connect up with existing private or public generating or transmission systems (where such facilities are available) or (b) to create an independent source of power is a question of policy or cost or convenience, or all three. Perhaps when first getting under way the preference would be given to connecting up with existing lines where fair prices for current can be secured. Independent sources of power might well be kept in the background.

But if it is decided to create a new source of power there are everywhere and always available Diesel engine installations and frequently local, or reachable, hydro-electric development sites. The electric current itself, in any case, can be made available to the rural population at a figure considerably below what is charged for it on existing rural lines. We here assume that the current can be made available at 2 cents or less per K.W.H.

Continued on page 62

DISTRIBUTION LINES

The cost of a mile of "high wire" line naturally depends on a number of variables, most important among them under normal conditions being the number of customers per mile and the method followed in doing the work; whether for instance it is piecemeal or large-scale construction. This cost of the line with transformers and meters included for one to three customers will range from $500 to $800 the mile. To amortize this cost in twenty years at 4 per cent involves a cost to each of three customers on a mile of line of about one dollar a month.

LARGE USE THE KEY TO LOW RATES

Real rural electrification implies large average use of current, for without large use rates cannot be made low enough to effect the coveted social advantages. Gifford Pinchot once said:

"Electricity in the home and on the farm must be made free—of course with a freedom of its own. We must work away from the point of view where we use it sparingly. Of course we should not waste it. But it is such a low-cost commodity that we must learn to substitute it for human labor. In this direction lies national economy. No intelligent person spares the use of water as a means to comfort and cleanliness—even though it costs enough to warrant its being metered. Water as a factor in our lives is free—not as free as air—but so free as to permit us to partake fully of its benefits."

The electrical industry because it secures over 60 per cent of its revenue from small consumers is all but stymied by its high-rate low-use situation. In planning for national rural electrification we must do everything to encourage the largest possible average use. Large average use, especially in the initial stages, seemingly requires a planning and investment beyond the capacity of a private company to initiate. Perhaps only the power and force of the Government can master the initial problem.

RATES

Both the form of electric rate schedules and the rates themselves vary widely throughout the United States. It has only recently been proven that most of these variations have little relation to cost. There will be variations in the cost of the rural electric service proposed. But how many of them are sufficiently important to recognize in rate variations is another matter. It is believed that charges as follows will quite generally cover costs for normal use:

A. $1.00 to $1.25 a month Connection Charge. Note: This is to pay for the line. Whenever the individual customer's share of the cost of the line is paid off this charge stops.

B. $1.00 a month Minimum Charge—includes 10 K.W.H.

C. 3 cents per K.W.H. for next 40 K.W.H.

D. 2 cents per K.W.H. balance

It would appear that under the expected consumptions the present average rural rate will certainly be cut in half.

DISTANCE BETWEEN FARMS

In the absence of a survey we can only approximate the mileage of line required to connect up any given number of customers. By a comparison state by state of the mileage of roads of all classes as furnished by the Bureau of Public Roads with the Census figures for the number of farms, the average number of farms per mile of road seems to vary from two to five to the mile. As the tendency will be first to electrify the most advantageous locations, three farms on the average to the mile can be used in making our estimates.

FINANCING OF LINES

If we connect up 500,000 farms not now having "high line" service we will more than double the number of connected "dirt farms" because a considerable percentage of the farms included in the Census figures are located in the neighborhood of large cities and are "farms" only in a very technical sense. The whole capital cost of rural electric service is divided between—

a. the cost of the distribution lines; and

b. the cost of the generating units required for areas which cannot be furnished current by the private companies.

For estimating purposes we have chosen units of 500,000 farms.

Mr. Otto M. Rau in estimates finds the costs of building lines for this number to be $112,000,000 or $225 the farm.

The Fairbanks, Morse Co. have given us an estimate of $262,000 for a generating unit to supply 1500 farms within a radius of ten miles. In many situations of course no new generating equipment will be needed. But to get the complete picture we can assume the wholly unlikely outcome that company service is nowhere available and that to serve a population of 500,000 divided into units of 1500 customers each, 333 such plants will be required at a total cost of $87,000,000.

Therefore to connect up 500,000 farms not now having service and providing current from power sources to be created anew would mean a capital outlay of $200,000,000 or $400 the farm. If one half of these farms could get current from existing sources the total outlay would be $150,000,000, or $300 the farm.

FEDERAL LEGAL SITUATION

It may be wise temporarily to utilize emergency legislation and funds to get this work started. However, there would appear to be no legal objection to organizing the work upon a permanent basis. A system of banks established expressly for the purpose could be set up, similar to existing Acts for the extension of agricultural credits, such as the Federal Land Bank Act of 1916. If it is desirable to operate by direct loans without the use of a special banking system, authority is found in the appropriating power of Congress under the so-called "general welfare" clause of the Constitution.

STATE LEGISLATIVE SITUATION

Present legislation in some states will act as a practical bar to rural electrification along the lines proposed. This is true in such states as Illinois and Pennsylvania which have no statutes authorizing the creation of power districts. Even here, however, the plan might be put into effect through farmers' mutuals operating without profit. In other states such as California and Nebraska adequate legislation exists and one hundred per cent co-operation would be possible.

A part of the plan would be to set up uniform state legislation and have the farmer-folk within the several states press for its adoption. Provision should be made for the incorporation of rural electric districts upon the favorable vote of a sufficient majority of inhabitants and/or of the owners of a sufficient majority of the acreage. Such districts should have power to acquire, construct and operate electric plants and to furnish electric service to their inhabitants and to others nearby. Provision should also be made for the organization of consumers' mutual electric companies. These electric service districts and consumers' mutual companies should receive Federal and/or State aid in the form of expert engineering, accounting and management advice, as farmers are now advised by experts in farm management, farm accounting, domestic science, farm crops, animal husbandry, fruit raising and the like.

Regions conspicuously without service should be investigated for determination of and report upon the advisability of Federal and/or State contributions toward the cost of rural lines such as are made by the Provincial Government of Ontario and in several European countries, and, if advisable, the methods to be followed in making such contributions.

THE ANSWER—A RURAL ELECTRIFICATION AGENCY

It is proposed to set up in the Department of the Interior—a section, manned by socially minded electrical engineers, who, having standardized rural electrification equipment, will cooperate with groups within the several states in planning appropriate developments. In many instances no Federal financing will be required. Where such schemes are self-liquidating financing in whole or in part may be provided. The possible bearing of proposed municipal power developments on rural electrification might properly influence allotments during the life of P.W.A. In fact the proposed Rural Electrification Section should take an active hand in planning out the rural use of current from such developments as Grand Coulee, Ft. Peck, Bonneville, Boulder Dam, Tygart Dam, etc. Cooperation with the Electric Home and Farm Authority would be an important function of the Rural Electrification Section.

—MORRIS LLEWELLYN COOKE

'I Hereby Establish . . .'

The "12-minute memo" was the document that convinced Ickes and Roosevelt of the desirability and "do-ability" of rural electrification. Other pressures spurred action. The American Farm Bureau Federation (AFBF) and the National Grange passed resolutions urging federal action to get light and power to the countryside. AFBF President Edward O'Neal told FDR: "Appoint this big boy from Philadelphia (Cooke) to advise you about rural electrification." The other pressure was the Depression itself. As unemployment held on stubbornly, Roosevelt sought and received $100 million for rural electrification as part of a $5 billion public works bill. The President then decided there ought to be a separate agency to administer what he first saw as a relief program. He had little trouble convincing the "big boy from Philadelphia" to head it. By the end of April, 1935, Cooke had set up makeshift operations in the basement of the Department of the Interior and was assembling staff. "This is to advise you that the Rural Electrification Unit is a going concern," he wrote FDR May 3. He closed by saying that he would have a suggested draft of the executive order setting up the Rural Electrification Administration early the next week. Roosevelt signed the order on May 11, 1935.

EXECUTIVE ORDER

ESTABLISHMENT OF THE RURAL ELECTRIFICATION ADMINISTRATION

By virtue of and pursuant to the authority vested in me under the Emergency Relief Appropriation Act of 1935, approved April 8, 1935 (Public Resolution No. 11, 74th Congress), I hereby establish an agency within the Government to be known as the "Rural Electrification Administration", the head thereof to be known as the Administrator.

I hereby prescribe the following duties and functions of the said Rural Electrification Administration to be exercised and performed by the Administrator thereof to be hereafter appointed:

To initiate, formulate, administer, and supervise a program of approved projects with respect to the generation, transmission, and distribution of electric energy in rural areas.

In the performance of such duties and functions, expenditures are hereby authorized for necessary supplies and equipment; law books and books of reference, directories, periodicals, newspapers and press clippings; travel expenses, including the expense of attendance at meetings when specifically authorized by the Administrator; rental at the seat of Government and elsewhere; purchase, operation and maintenance of passenger-carrying vehicles; printing and binding; and incidental expenses; and I hereby authorize the Administrator to accept and utilize such voluntary and uncompensated services and, with the consent of the State, such State and local officers and employees, and appoint, without regard to the provisions of the civil service laws, such officers and employees, as may be necessary, prescribe their duties and responsibilities and, without regard to the Classification Act of 1923, as amended, fix their compensation: **Provided,** *That in so far as practicable, the persons employed under the authority of this Executive Order shall be selected from those receiving relief.*

To the extent necessary to carry out the provisions of this Executive Order the Administrator is authorized to acquire, by purchase or by the power of eminent domain, any real property or any interest therein and improve, develop, grant, sell, lease (with or without the privilege of purchasing), or otherwise dispose of any such property or interest therein.

For the administrative expenses of the Rural Electrification Administration there is hereby allocated to the Administration from the appropriation made by the Emergency Relief Appropriation Act of 1935 the sum of $75,000. Allocations will be made hereafter for authorized projects.

Franklin D Roosevelt

The White House,
May 11, 1935

7037

1

Above: Executive Order 7037, which created REA. Below: Cooke (center), with Relief Administrator Harry Hopkins (left) and Interior Secretary Harold L. Ickes, after a May 2, 1935, White House conference on the new program for rural electrification.

2

A many-gabled mansion just off Washington's Dupont Circle became the unlikely headquarters for the modern program of rural electrification. As REA's staff grew, it had eight other "satellite" locations in town houses nearby.

REA Administrator Cooke had held out hope for industry participation in the big job of electrifying rural areas. He played out that string to the end, but as 1935 closed, the flood of applications on his desk for REA loans indicated the "program" was going to be executed along cooperative lines.

1

2

An awesome task lay before the little agency. The REA was entrusted with electrifying more than five million farms. Only 10.9 percent of all farms had central station service. These were the most affluent farmers or farms near towns. The electric industry, through the Committee on the Relation of Electricity to Agriculture (CREA), had been working on the problem since the 1920s. Important pioneering research was produced by CREA, but the chief barrier—prohibitive costs and rates—still kept most of rural America in the dark, powerless.

3

4

5

6

More than 500 rural residents of Miami and Shelby Counties in Ohio gathered at the Piqua Municipal Light Plant on November 14, 1935, to participate in the setting of the first pole for construction of power lines by Miami Rural Electric Cooperative. Newly organized by the Ohio Farm Bureau, the co-op would construct 193 miles of line with a $250,000 REA loan. Participants who could be identified from left, are: Murray D. Lincoln, Ohio Farm Bureau executive secretary; REA publicist Dorothy Moore; W.R. Joslin, president of Shelby County Rural Electric Membership Corp. (with shovel); M.O. Swanson, REA chief engineer; Mrs. Emmett P. Brush, "representing the women of the county"; Leonard J. Coate, Miami director; and Leonard U. Hill, president, Miami Electric (with shovel). The two co-ops later merged as Pioneer Rural Electric Cooperative.

REA's First Year

By late May of 1935, the makeshift operations of REA, still considered the rural electrification "unit" of the federal relief program, had moved to the George Westinghouse, Jr., mansion at 2000 Massachusetts Avenue, just off Washington's Dupont Circle.

There followed several months of feverish activity when vital REA policies were established that continue to this day.

Cooke assembled a competent—and enthusiastic—REA staff. Heated discussions went on into the nights about the unworkability of REA as a relief agency. The Emergency Relief Appropriation Act required that at least 25 percent of funds be spent directly for labor and that 90 percent of that labor should be taken from the unemployed relief rolls. REA soon determined that power lines could not be built with unskilled labor. Upon advice of Cooke, Roosevelt took the agency out of the relief business and made it a lending agency, establishing the federal pattern that was to electrify rural America.

It was during those formative months that Cooke's eyes were opened as to the willingness of the privately owned utilities to work with REA. He met with top power company leaders in May and asked them for a proposal on how they would proceed with REA loans in a national rural electrification plan. They returned with a plan in July. Cooke was more than disappointed—he was outraged. The report proposed that the utilities take the entire $100 million REA appropriations for loan funds to connect 351,000 prospective rural customers. These were the "cream" of the rural business, the large and easy-to-connect users—only 247,000 of them farmers. These were the "very few farms requiring electricity for major farm operations that are now not served," according to the companies. What about the other five million farms, Cooke wanted to know.

Meanwhile, loan applications poured in by the hundreds and inquiries by the thousands. Many came from farm organizations and cooperatives. The REA staff was divided over the inexperienced co-ops' applications—most strongly against, but a few strongly for them. Cooke himself was ambivalent, but as the months wore on, he saw the handwriting on the wall. By December of 1935, it was apparent that the farm co-ops were forging to the front as the primary borrowers under the REA program.

The Rural Electrification Act

At the end of 1935 REA was still plagued by problems because of its status as a relief agency. With funding for loans appropriated by Congress under emergency conditions, monies could be taken away by "whims and trims."

Senator George W. Norris of Nebraska, a long-time legislative friend and ally of Administrator Cooke, was convinced that rural electrification in America would never be accomplished without REA receiving regular appropriations and full status as a government agency.

In early January of 1936, Norris and Representative Sam Rayburn of Texas introduced similar bills in the Senate and the House. They called for REA to be set up as an independent agency and authorized it to make loans for rural electrification with preference to "States, Territories, and subdivisions and agencies, thereof, municipalities, people's utility districts and cooperative, nonprofit or limited dividend associations."

The legislation received a less hostile reception in the Senate than it did in the House of Representatives, where it was reported out of Rep. Rayburn's committee by a margin of only one vote.

The Senate Agriculture Committee had not held hearings. Norris, the committee's senior minority member, explained why with aplomb in a floor speech, February 25, 1936:

"There are all kinds of organizations in almost every State in the Union—farmers' organizations, consumers' organizations, commercial organizations—which would have been glad to appear; but they were all in favor of the bill."

The measure finally cleared both chambers on voice votes, and following lengthy and often heated conference committee discussions, it was approved. President Roosevelt signed it on May 21, 1936—one year and ten days after the Rural Electrification Administration had been created by executive order.

1 *Representative Rayburn*

2 *Senator Norris*

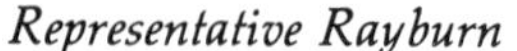

'The Act': A Legislative History

Jan. 6, 1936—Senator Norris of Nebraska and Rep. Rayburn of Texas introduce bills calling for a permanent REA, S. 3483 and H.R. 9681.

Feb. 17—Senate Committee on Agriculture and Forestry reports Norris bill with amendments.

Feb. 25 and 26, and March 4 and 5—Senate debates S. 3483.

March 5—Senate passes S. 3483 amended.

March 12, 13, and 14—House Committee on Interstate and Foreign Commerce holds hearings on S. 3483.

March 23—House Committee on Interstate and Foreign Commerce reports S. 3483, with amendments.

April 9—House debates and passes the amended bill.

April 10—Senate disagrees with House amendments and names conferees.

April 13—House insists upon its amendments and names conferees.

May 14—Conference report submitted to House, debated and approved.

May 15—Conference report approved by Senate.

May 21—President signs Rural Electrification Act of 1936.

3

'I Am Opposed'

"I am opposed to the Federal Government's going into the power business or lending money for the purpose of generating electricity."

—Senator William H. King of Utah, leader of Senate opposition to RE bill, February 26, 1936

'Economic Greed'

"So long as we look at the matter of rural electrification in the light of economic greed, private profit, and speculation, nothing will ever be done for the farmer."

—Rep. Murray Maverick of Texas, a leading proponent of the RE bill, April 9, 1936

4

5

Artist's rendition reconstructing April 9 debate shows Rep. Schuyler Merritt (left) in heated exchange with fiery Rep. John Rankin (right). Rep. Sam Rayburn, at Rankin's right, watches intently.

'I Do Not Care to Give This Gentleman More Time'

The most heated debate on the passage of the Rural Electrification Act took place on the floor of the House of Representatives.

The chief House defender proved to be Mississippi's John Elliot Rankin. When Connecticut's Schuyler Merritt rose to defend the "progress" the private utilities had made in electrifying rural America, Rankin took him on:

Rankin: The gentleman says electric service is quite new. Of course it is no more new in this country than in Europe.

Merritt: If you compare [Europe] with the Eastern states or California, I think the results are as satisfactory here as they are there.

Rankin: I wonder if the gentleman knows that in New Zealand two-thirds of their farms are electrified, [and] in the United States 10 percent are. . . .

Merritt: In New Zealand they deal with enormous tracts of land. . . . Also, New Zealand is a socialistic state.

Rankin: I wonder if the gentleman knows that in France and Germany 90 percent of their farms are electrified. Those are not socialistic states.

Merritt: No, they are not socialistic, but they are imperialistic.

Rankin: I wonder if the gentleman knows that Holland and Switzerland are practically 100 percent electrified.

Merritt: But they are no larger than our New England.

Rankin: I understand that there is no state in New England that has even 25 percent of its rural farms electrified.

Merritt: I do not care to give this gentleman more time.

'He Stands Forth as the Very Perfect, Gentle Knight of American Progressive Ideals'

The above words were spoken about George William Norris by Franklin Roosevelt on September 29, 1932, in McCook, Nebraska. They echo the conclusion of history and of his colleagues: Norris is honored as much for his character and human qualities as for his accomplishments.

On another occasion, Roosevelt perhaps came as close as anyone to assessing Norris' qualities when he told the Senator:

Senator Norris, I go along with you because you follow in their footsteps. You are radical, like Jefferson, a demagog like Jackson, an idealist like Lincoln, a theorist like Wilson, wild like Theodore Roosevelt. You dare to be all things.

Rural Americans are indebted to Norris because he "dared to be all things"—and because he dared to dream the great dream of bringing the light and power to the land.

He was the principal author of the legislation creating the Tennessee Valley Authority in 1933, a forerunner of rural electrification in America. And, although he is marked in history as one of America's truly great and progressive national legislators, the people of rural electrification remember him today as the legislative "father" of the Rural Electrification Act of 1936.

1

Rural electrification, the interests of the electric consumer, and the needs of the American farmer were essential elements of the progressive agenda which George Norris pursued relentlessly and fearlessly in his 40 years of distinguished public service in the U.S. Congress.

2

Senator Norris and Congressman John E. Rankin were speakers at REA's sixth birthday dinner, May, 1941.

3

A four-cent commemorative stamp honoring Senator Norris was issued in 1961 for the centennial observance of his birth.

4

The independent Norris (at microphone) campaigning successfully for a fifth term in the U.S. Senate. President Franklin D. Roosevelt (second from right), supporting Norris at the October, 1936, appearance in Omaha, told Nebraskans, "George Norris' candidacy transcends state and party lines." At far right is Texas Congressman Murray Maverick, a Democrat. Man in center is unidentified.

George Norris: His Straight Line of Duty

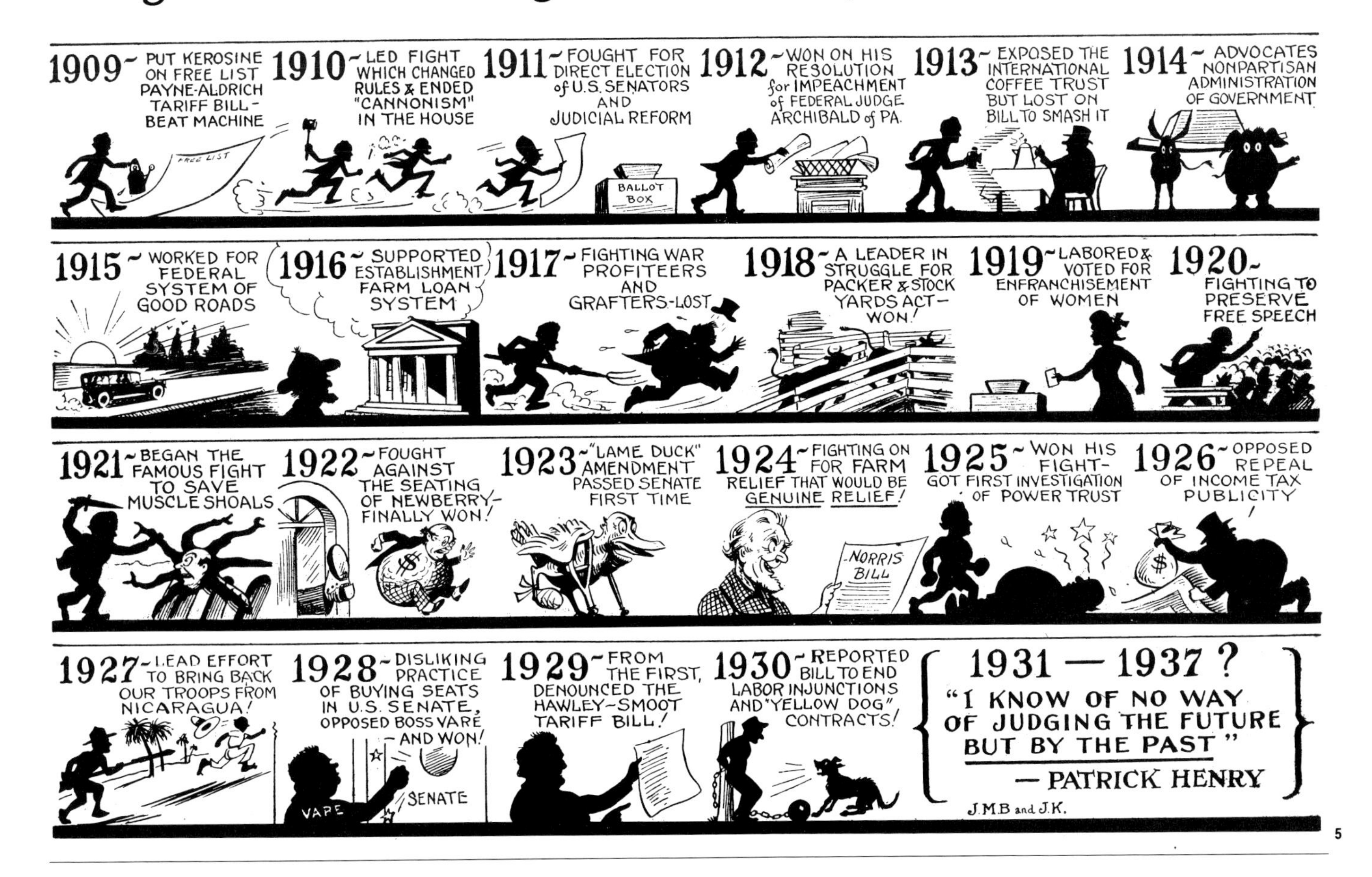

5

REA Administrator Morris L. Cooke itemizing tasks for his "detail" man, Deputy Administrator John M. Carmody. Cooke was the architect of policy of the rural power program, Carmody its master of "method." As Cooke's successor, Carmody was to become the "great line builder."

REA Staff: 'The Best and the Brightest'

Passage of the Rural Electrification Act of 1936, with provisions for allotments earmarked for each state, spurred loan applications. REA was swamped in an avalanche of requests.

The Depression had made it possible for REA to attract and employ "the best and the brightest" of engineers, accountants, lawyers, and other specialists and technicians.

As the thrust and outlines of the REA program emerged, Cooke saw a need for the agency to train its own people. He recruited the cream of the nation's leading engineering schools, gave these top achievers a full year's training, then assigned them regular positions.

John Carmody, REA's deputy administrator for organization, took the helm from Administrator Cooke in early 1937 after the exhausted Cooke was convinced the agency and the rural electrification program now had "a life of its own." Indeed, it did, as the energetic Carmody was later to recall:

Things really got rolling in 1937. The program was alive. Enthusiasm ran high in REA and throughout rural areas. Buried projects were dug out of many desks. The status of every project from application to construction was put on the table in full view of the entire staff for examination. We had weekly production meetings.

Cooke and Carmody themselves were among the world's best industrial engineers, but they called on others in that profession to help them. Leading consultants, like H.S. Person, internationally recognized in his field, were retained to develop sound management principles and practices for REA. Later, this expertise and advice would go outward to the cooperatives, their engineers and contractors.

One employee described what it was like to be there, to have the "REA feeling":

"There was not only a high degree of skill, but a certain enthusiasm, a missionary spirit, a freedom from subservience to old ideas or antagonistic interests."

Washington gossip also had it that an applicant for a job there had to have a "pure and pasteurized" public philosophy to join the REA staff. "Pure and pasteurized," that is, according to Cooke and Carmody.

2

Carmody brought Col. George D. Babcock to REA as "Engineer in Management" to put assembly line methods to work. He slashed the time between loan approvals and awarding of contracts from 36 to 12 weeks.

3

Energy and power leaders from around the world toured the REA electrified farm of Rosedale outside Washington in September, 1936. The exhibit was part of the Third World Power Conference, which had taken up rural electrification in a serious way.

Top achievers from the nation's leading engineering schools were screened and selected to work at REA. This early group, which included a number of the agency's later outstanding staff members, was photographed in January, 1937. Ready to tackle the big job of electrifying America's rural areas are standing, from left: James M. McCutchen, Edward E. Warner, Reginald E. Cole, William E. Trommershausen, John K. Taylor, Hoburg B. Lee, Ellsworth J. Johnson, J. Emmett Judge, Bruce O. Watkins, Edward E. Combs, Jr., George K. Ditlow and William J. Hauck. Seated, from left, are Herman Harms, Jr., Ellis A. Ceander, John W. Flanagan and Earl F. Clark.

4

1

Two years after President Roosevelt's executive order creating REA, agency publicists congratulated themselves on progress. Deputy Administrator Carmody had earlier ordered a halt to releasing stories of "marvelous progress" until there really were some. Now they could "PR" the program with complete justification.

Carmody presided over weekly top-level staff meetings where projects and progress were rigorously reviewed. From left: Chief Engineer M.O. Swanson; Regional Engineer Ben Creim (Pacific and Mountain West); Ward B. Freeman, chief, project control; Col. George W. Babcock, industrial management consultant (at window); Administrator Carmody; and T.E. O'Callaghan, assistant general counsel. Staff members to O'Callaghan's left are unidentified.

2

3

In its first year the REA staff resolved critical policy and procedural issues. The "program" then got its bearings and "took off" in early 1937. Construction progress in this illustrated REA chart is measured in thousands of miles.

4

REA Administrator John M. Carmody, with Mrs. Carmody, pressed a telegraph key in Washington which gave the signal for the energization of the lines of Darke County Rural Electric Cooperative, Greenville, Ohio. The lines were energized on May 11, 1938—REA's third birthday.

REA Gets Rolling

The loan applications mounted. And by 1938, the lights were burning brightly into the nights at 2000 Massachusetts (and eight other locations) near Dupont Circle as the staff of REA, now at more than 600, struggled to meet demands. The staff was putting in so many long hours that Carmody called a meeting to insist that employees work fewer hours. There had been several cases of auto accidents after REA people fell asleep at the wheel.

Making a decision to provide more direct management assistance to the inexperienced and newly formed co-ops, Carmody brought on more staff and also brought to bear all that he had known and experienced in his considerable years of management. He felt that the production controls so effective in factories could also be applied to REA operations. He devised a "paperwork factory," a plan to streamline the administration of the loans. Col. George Babcock, who had designed one of the early car assembly lines, was brought in to develop a streamlined system. There were deadlines, "log-in" and "log-out" procedures, weekly production meetings. Shaving the weeks, days and hours off loan processing, while maintaining the high standards, became a competitive "game" among the REA employees. Down, down, down went the time between loan approval and awarding of construction contracts—from 36 weeks in 1936 to 12 by early 1939.

In July, 1939, Carmody resigned from the agency to become Federal Works Administrator. In his 28 months of leadership, over 100,000 miles of REA-financed power line had been completed and more than one million rural people had received electricity for the first time.

On January 1, 1940, Carmody's successor, REA Administrator Harry Slattery, was able to report to Congress that REA had financed and made possible in a short four-and-one-half years the energizing of 180,000 miles of power line with another 80,000 miles under construction or in various stages of planning.

The brilliant REA staff's work extended on down to the drafting table and the blueprint for cutting costs and expediting rural electrification's reach and spread across the land. Two of REA's "best and brightest" work on a system-wide electric distribution plan utilizing the new single-phase construction methods.

Simplicity of design and standardization of materials—with consequent reduced cost of service to the consumer—characterized specifications for the REA projects developed by the REA engineers.

1

1. *Old type single-phase construction*
2. *REA single-phase construction*
3. *Conversion of REA 1-phase to 3-phase line by addition of cross-arm*

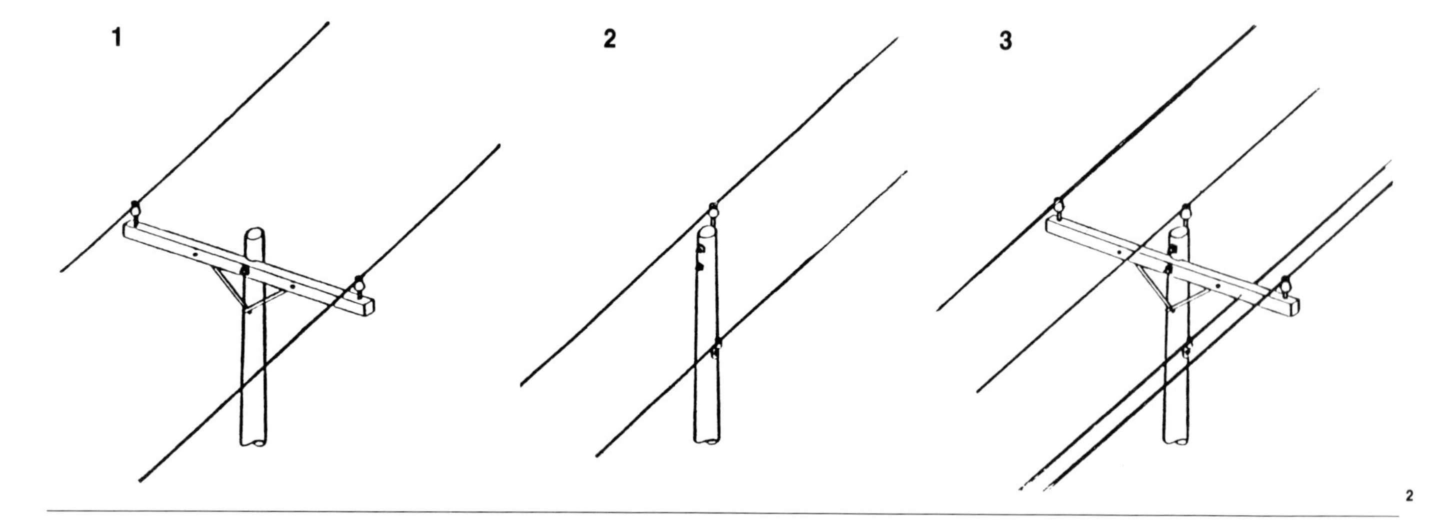

2

3

These three pioneering REA engineers, devising and planning on the "system-wide" basis, were key to the successful development of the assembly-line construction method that accelerated rural line construction and reduced costs. From left, they are Henry Richter, REA design engineer; M.O. Swanson, chief engineer; and Col. C.W. Sass, assistant chief engineer.

4

By the late 1930s, the single-phase lines along a rural road signaled that REA and rural electrification were "on the march." The single-phase construction method developed by REA, combined with other innovations and economies, hastened the spread of the lines to the farms. Steadily declining costs translated into REA projects becoming "do-able" for the farmers and their co-ops.

REA Innovates, Results Electrifying

Since the days of the Giant Power study and the later survey in New York State, Morris Cooke and rural electrification's pioneering engineers had the "hard numbers" to show that costs of rural power lines had been kept artificially high.

Now they set out to prove that costs could be driven down dramatically. Resourceful engineers and management specialists used a creative combination of innovations to achieve their goal.

One was the use of high-strength conductors, newly introduced in the industry. These permitted longer spans, reducing the number of poles per mile from about 30 to 18.

Another was REA's development of a single-phase line with light and tough poles minus the then-familiar cross-arms.

A third was system-wide planning instead of the old pole-by-pole approach. They put construction on an assembly-line basis.

Manufacturers followed their designs and contractors, using REA "specs," began to erect lines that were not only cheaper, simpler and lighter, but also "tough"—able to withstand severe punishment from the elements.

As REA-financed construction accelerated, large-scale bidding and purchases, the assembly-line technique and its waves of workmen performing specialized tasks down the country roads—and the standardized hardware—all came together to dramatically drive costs down.

By 1939, the average mile of rural line cost only $538 to build. Even with all the "overhead" added in, the cost was still only $825. Previously, it had ranged between $1,500 and $2,000.

By the late 1930s, the single-phase lines along a rural road signaled that REA and rural electrification were "on the march."

The awesome technical and management skills of the early REA engineers and other specialists set a pattern of high standards and commitment to low-cost rural power that has become almost legendary. Their contribution to the success of rural electrification was enormous.

1

2

President Roosevelt addressed a crowd of 40,000 in the open-air stadium of Gordon Military College at Barnesville, Georgia. Occasion was the energization of lines of Lamar Electric Membership Corporation. His rural electrification program, begun rather haltingly only three years before, was now a stunning success. He was proud of it.

3

4

5

FDR was at turns the national leader, head of his party, then Georgia neighbor. He talked about his plans for economic development, put in good words for his favorite congressional candidates, then told the story of how Georgia was the birthplace of his idea to electrify rural areas. It was at his rural cottage in Warm Springs, he told the crowd, that he found his electric bill too high, decided to do something about it nationwide.

6

REA's Carmody, urging co-op director-control, cautioned against lawyers and engineers "assuming command" and said women should "take a more active part in management."

FDR Shares a Story

With 40,000 Georgians massed before him, President Roosevelt looked out over the crowd in the flag-decked open stadium of Gordon Military College at Barnesville. It was August 11, 1938, and the occasion was the dedication of lines of Lamar Electric Membership Corporation. Holding himself upright and gripping the podium firmly, he leaned forward and shared a warm and human story with his Georgia friends:

"Fourteen years ago a Democratic Yankee came to a neighboring county in your state in search of a pool of warm water wherein he might swim his way back to health. The place—Warm Springs—was a rather dilapidated, small summer resort. His new neighbors extended to him the hand of genuine hospitality, welcomed him to their firesides and made him feel so much at home that he built himself a house, bought himself a farm, and has been coming back ever since.

"There was only one discordant note in that first stay of mine at Warm Springs: When the first-of-the-month bill came in for electric light for my little cottage, I found that the charge was 18 cents a kilowatt-hour—about four times as much as I paid in Hyde Park, New York. That started my long study of proper public-utility charges for electric current and the whole subject of getting electricity into farm homes.

"So it can be said that a little cottage at Warm Springs, Georgia, was the birthplace of the Rural Electrification Administration.

"Electricity is a modern necessity of life and ought to be found in every village, every home, and every farm in every part of the United States. The dedication of this Rural Electrification Administration project in Georgia is a symbol of the progress we are making—and we are not going to stop."

RURAL ELECTRIFICATION ADMINISTRATION · U. S. DEPT. OF AGRICULT

IT'S COMING—

ELECTRICITY

FOR YOU

The People, Yes

The people . . . will stick around a long time. The people run the works, only they don't know it yet—you wait and see.

In his epic poem, *The People, Yes,* the prairie poet Carl Sandburg echoes the voices and moods of the American people of the late 1930s. The words above were spoken by a Minnesota farm wife to her husband.

That farm wife could well have been one of those tens of thousands in rural America who were ready to "run the works."

She, like her neighbors, had heard that REA and the co-ops were bringing electricity to rural America.

Now farm wives throughout the country were nudging their uncertain husbands to come up with the $5 membership fee—to "sign up to get the REA." Sign up and get an iron, a radio, washing machine, power tools. . . .

1

Cooperativeness, one of the higher and creative impulses in human nature, was practiced in rural society as "the neighborly thing to do." Applied beyond the neighborhood to rural enterprise, co-ops in rural America, and worldwide, practiced these principles:

Democratic control or one member-one vote.

Open membership, no discrimination.

Limited return on investment, emphasizing service and financial health, rather than profit.

Return of savings, or margins, in proportion to members' patronage.

Education, education, education—in the cooperative way and philosophy.

Cooperation among cooperatives.

2

3

4

The Co-op Idea

The adversities of farm life and work—severe weather, faltering economics, awesome distances, extreme isolation—had made rural Americans at once natural and necessary cooperators.

From barn raisings, threshing bees and quilting bees to co-op creameries and grain elevators, they joined to accomplish what one could not do alone but what many could do together.

But when the idea of rural electrification through cooperatives first reached rural America it met some skepticism. Farm families understood using cooperatives to meet their supply or marketing needs. But an electric co-op?

Fear of the unknown made farmers think twice about going into something that mysterious. Electricity wasn't like wheat or fertilizer that could be held in the hand and looked at. It came from far away over humming lines. And you needed engineers and lawyers to tame it.

But in spite of the enormity and the complexity of it all, the co-op idea—in partnership with REA—became the dynamic force which carried rural America out of darkness.

The Sign-Up

The work fell to a handful of leaders, the faithful few, who saw the potential and carried the message. Once they got started, there was no stopping them.

Working without pay, they went from farm to farm and galvanized the resolve of their neighbors and friends to "get lights" on a co-op basis.

Once the word got out in a rural area that an REA co-op was being organized, the first meeting would bring a stampede of applicants. More meetings would follow, sometimes one every night.

Finally, the organizing committee would call a halt to the meetings, get out the county road maps and begin to "plot in" the homes of the people who had signed up. Usually, with the help of an REA field man, the committee would draw lines where they thought the wires could be strung, picking up as many new members as possible. Distinctive marks were given to schoolhouses, churches, filling stations, grain elevators and stores.

When they had a general idea of the path of the proposed lines, they split into pairs to call personally on those farmers along the line who had not yet joined.

Rural people were not universal in their demand for electricity. Some worried about "getting in debt to the government." A few were not sure that electricity was worth the expense. And, in the 1930s, $5 was a sum not to be taken lightly.

The sign-up teams got wiser as they went along. They found it better to have the farmer's wife present when they talked about the benefits of electricity. They looked at her when they talked about lights to help the children study or

1

2

1

PETITION McLean, Shelby

We, the undersigned, being deeply interested in the matter of obtaining electric energy in the community in which we reside, and particularly on our own roads, do hereby petition the Ohio Farm Bureau Federation to exercise every effort possible to aid us in obtaining electricity in this community. We urge the Ohio Farm Bureau Federation to obtain all available information, including surveys if possible, relative to the availability of electric lines in our community. It is understood that this obligates us in no way except to show that we are interested, and we pledge our support and assistance in every way possible in the furthering of this enterprise.

NAME	ADDRESS
Ed B. [illegible]	Fort Loramie Ohio
Fred H. Helgefort	" " "
Jos. H[illegible]	
Henry J Borchers	
Herman Poeppelman	
Bernard Schlater	Ft. Loramie Ohio

Please draw on back a sketch of the roads covered, approximate mileage of these roads, and number of residences (both of those interested and others.)

2

3

How the rural areas were electrified is one of the greatest achievements of cooperative and economic democracy this nation has ever known. In the late 1930s and early 1940s, farm men and women all over America went up and down the country roads—petitioning, organizing, electing—for power. They met. They planned. They built. The entire process of securing signatures, the "sign-ups," the pledge of land for the lines, was a test of rural citizens and their leaders, of their collective resolve to attain the long-denied power. Most met that test and more. They would learn about the mysteries of electricity later. Now it was their cooperative savvy and skills, their great desire, that made the difference: "Mr. Carmody, We Want Lights."

4

5

6

DIX
BROWN
EAST BEND
LUDLOW
HARWOOD
MIDDLE FORK
BLUE RIDGE
CONDIT
RANTOUL
SOMER
CARROLL

1

GRUNDY COUNTY R.E.A.

2

3

when they described electric refrigeration. Often the wife would pay the sign-up fee before the organizers had finished arguing with the husband. Sometimes, the teams had women members. Like "Granny." Said one balking farmer who was finally convinced: "If such a sweet little old lady is so dead set on it, why I guess I'll go along."

Then began the easement campaign. At the outset of the electric program, REA did not approve use of funds to purchase rights-of-way over farmlands. The co-op organizers had to obtain thousands of easements across property, each one signed by the owner. Some idea of the size of the task was indicated by organizers collecting more than one million separate easements by 1941.

The job would have been difficult enough had all farmers been agreeable, but many were not. They had first been sold on the co-op idea, then persuaded to put up $5 to sign up. Finally they were asked to part with a strip of their land. Most did, though some balked, at least at first.

Then there were those who wanted electricity but could not be included in the first construction phase. They were too far from the main line, or they lived in areas where not enough neighbors had signed up. A line had to pay its way or it couldn't be built. REA had determined that this meant three hookups per mile, a rule Congress would later liberalize.

One farmer was told his home was too far from the electric line. A few days later he returned, waving his $5.

"I moved my house," he said in triumph.

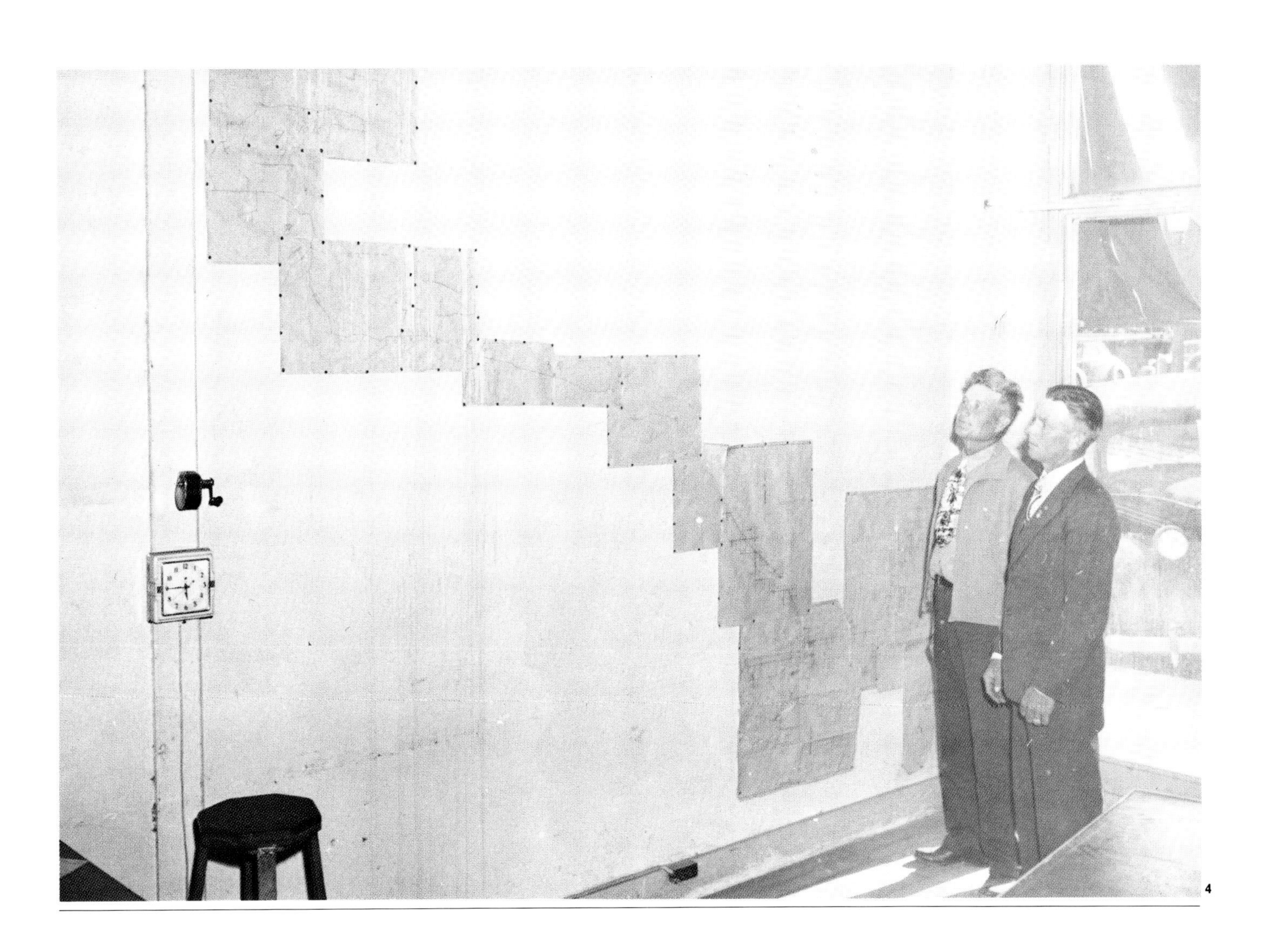
4

1

2

'And Some Died Aborning'

Sometimes the plan didn't work out. The sign-up would be completed, but a co-op's members would wake up to discover that overnight the local power company had built a power line right through the heart of their service area.

The company had "skimmed the cream," hooking up the easy-to-reach farms and businesses in the most densely settled areas—areas the co-op had counted on to make the whole system "pay out."

The incidents were not isolated. A 1940 REA survey showed there had been some 200 cases of "spite-line" or "cream-skimming" activities in 38 states since 1936. Eight newly organized cooperatives were wiped out entirely; many others were considerably weakened.

REA Cooperative Specialist Udo Rall recalled the "trouble" in 1953:

"In the mountains of central Pennsylvania is a fertile valley, perhaps five miles wide and 20 miles long, hemmed in by rugged hills and reached only by a narrow pass. . . . A co-op made preparations to serve that valley, even staking the lines. The power company . . . then built lines through the pass.

"In Virginia, a co-op engineered a line north through the wilderness, ending in a prosperous dairy section near Chancellorsville. When construction was about to start, the power company built a short line out of Chancellorsville to serve a handful of the large-consumption dairies on which the co-op had counted to make its 40 miles of line feasible.

"Such cream skimming and spite lines hurt new electric co-ops badly. Of the two loans on which REA has taken a loss, one was to a co-op in New York which was spite-lined to death. . . .

"Others hurt by such tactics are still in operation, but they are less strong than if they had encountered fair play.

"And some died aborning."

Direct intervention by farmers was important to co-ops like Adams Electric, Gettysburg, Pennsylvania, which got its start out of the local Farm Bureau office (right). Friday, *a now-defunct photo magazine, told the Adams story in its April, 1941, issue by reconstructing how co-op members took matters into their own hands. Shown in silhouette (far left) are two farmers sawing off a Pennsylvania Power and Light Company (PP&L) pole near the farm of R. Boyd McCullough (middle right), who refused PP&L entry over his land. At left, farmers assembling at the historic Big Spring Mill near Gettysburg on January 30, 1941, to follow behind PP&L crews with shovels, filling in freshly dug holes. Commonwealth officials stepped in, arbitrating a favorable settlement for the co-op. Spite lines appeared in many regions, as the letter and map below indicate.*

3

CENTRAL ALABAMA ELECTRIC MEMBERSHIP CORPORATION
(A FEDERAL RURAL ELECTRIFICATION PROJECT)
PRATTVILLE, ALABAMA

DIRECTORS:
MAURY A. McWILLIAMS (AUTAUGA) PRATTVILLE
J. MAX ROGERS (COOSA) RT. 4, GOODWATER
C. C. HALL (ELMORE) RT. 1, TITUS
MRS. GORDON DeRAMUS (AUTAUGA) BOOTH
C. C. KING (AUTAUGA) JONES
DONALD ROBBINS (COOSA) GOODWATER
N. H. HARRELL (CHILTON) BILLINGSLEY
S. D. DeLOACH (CHILTON) RT. 2, VERBENA
SETH JOHNSON, JR. (ELMORE) RT. 4, WETUMPKA

PROJECT SUPERINTENDENT
BASIL THOMPSON
PRATTVILLE, ALABAMA

November 22, 1941

NOV 24

Rural Electrification Administration
Att. Mr. W. P. Coppinger

Dear Mr. Coppinger:

In answer to your telegram dated November 1, with reference to the Alabama Power Company constructing a line which was discussed at the state wide meeting November 12, we enclose herewith drawing which shows facts in the case.

From the enclosed drawing you will note that a primary line has been constructed to serve one consumer with a distance of 2052 feet and a service of 50 feet. This line was constructed to serve Mr. J. I. Moon and is located 2½ miles south of Clanton, Alabama. According to Mr. Moon's statement the line was energized on November 11, 1941.

Hoping that this covers the information that you desired.

Very truly yours

Basil Thompson

Basil Thompson
Project Supt.
Ala. 30 Autauga

WCW/jd

4

5

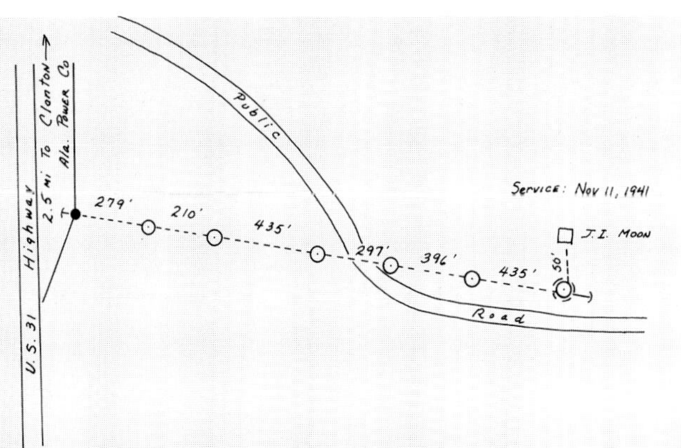

6

The Lines Go Up

REA's "moving belt" assembly-line technique revolutionized rural line construction. Instead of a crew standing fixed alongside a moving assembly line as in a factory, the rural roadway stood still and waves of workmen, broken down into specialized crews, moved along it.

REA's first chief engineer, M.O. Swanson, described an early version of the technique to a farm audience in 1936:

"First come two men with a tape, a load of stakes and some paint. They measure off the pole spacing. They quickly appraise the local conditions, paint a few symbols on a stake and drive it into the ground. Repeating this process, they move on down the line.

"Pretty soon a truck loaded with the poles comes along. The driver and his helper read the symbols on the stake: '35-B-18-X.'

"Then comes the assembly truck. The driver reads the stake's message, 'Let's see, 35-B-18-X. Here we are.' He unloads insulators, nuts and bolts, a transformer, guys and anchors.

"Next comes the post-hole diggers and mechanics. The stake tells the diggers where the hole should be dug, and it tells the mechanics what hardware should be attached to the pole.

"Then a gang of men with pike poles and equipment follow, quickly setting the pole in place.

"Then comes the truck to string the conductors. As it moves along, the linemen secure the conductors, hang the transformers and otherwise prepare the line for service.

"This is real standardization—the assembly-line idea applied to rural electric line construction."

1

2

Early line crews were often made up of unskilled workers taken from the employment rolls or farmers who would join cooperatively to get the job done. Aided with few power tools and with little method applied to the task, erection of the lines were sometimes primitive affairs. But after 1935, REA developed assembly-line methods for constructing lines with uniform procedures and standardized types of electrical hardware. The results were lowered costs which made rural electrification economically feasible for more and more cooperatives. The number and rate of REA projects accelerated.

3

4

5

1

2

3

The photo at above left, unquestionably the most widely published in rural electrification, captures high drama and momentum as the last miles of line are pulled only the day before energization for Brown-Atchison Electric Cooperative Association, Horton, Kansas, on March 31, 1938. Crew members on the truck were local farmers hired by a Kansas City, Missouri, contractor; wages earned by the farmer-linemen went to wire their farm homes. Crew members from left to right are: Glynn Jacobson, Junior Adams, Elmer Krebs and Carl Jacobson, all destined to become legend as rural electrification's "Four Horsemen of the Lines." Photo of the wire-stringing crew (above right) has not been paired with its "twin" since April, 1938.

The unidentified photos at lower left and right are from early REA files and are thought to be of a crew erecting poles and lines on a federal relief project, possibly before 1935.

4

1 2 3 4

5

Not always did the work go smoothly. Invariably obstacles presented plenty of opportunity for imagination by contractors.

One resourceful builder found it impossible to drive his pole truck through muddy fields, so he hitched a trailer to his truck and hauled a mule in it. When his crew hit mud, the mule was unloaded, hitched to a pole, and the beast pulled the pole into position for the pole-setters.

Construction also had its dramatic moments.

In the summer of 1939, an Indiana woman lay dying of pneumonia in her farmhouse. The doctor said that an oxygen tent might save her, but there was no electricity in the house to operate the tent fan. Three linemen, working in a driving rainstorm, built a 500-foot extension in just two hours. The switch was turned on and the woman's life was saved.

Many reports flowing into REA's Washington offices from the co-ops and contractors related unusual difficulties and adversities met and overcome. Generally, these accounts were matter-of-fact and cast in technical language. But no matter how dry the report, it was impossible to miss the sense of satisfaction and pride. And contractors and crews got an extra reward: They witnessed farm families getting lights for the first time.

6

7

Ready for the 'Zero Hour'

Once the electric lines moved out into the countryside and farms began to be hooked up, families quickly prepared for the new helper.

"Group wiring plans" let co-op members join together to get their places wired before the lines were energized, keeping the cost to $55.

On the Great Plains, the co-ops advanced money for farmers to buy wire and fixtures. A master wireman would be hired to take orders and to offer advice, and farmers would buy materials at cost plus ten percent and hire journeymen to do the work.

Manufacturers, working with REA, put out "lighting packages" at prices that seemed incredibly low, even then. Each package contained nine modern fixtures and sold for about $18.

The 1938 report of a superintendent of an REA project in Michigan describes the excitement of it all:

"I could take you to hundreds of homes completely wired, with fixtures hung and bulbs in place, ready for the 'zero hour' when the lines will first be energized. I could take you to homes where electric ranges, electric refrigerators, radios and even electric clocks are installed and ready for operation. I could show you . . . "

1

2

3

4

In most cases the new rural electric consumers heeded the advice of the REA and their local co-op and went ahead and had the house wired before the lines were energized. That done, they would purchase as many appliances as they could afford in readiness for the big day. Once the house was electrically outfitted, power equipment for the farm was the next big step. Promotional efforts (opposite page) by the agency, often entertaining, helped extend electric power to rural America.

1

'We Didn't Want to Miss It'

I wanted to be at my parents' house when electricity came. It was in 1940. We'd all go around flipping the switch, to make sure it hadn't come on yet. We didn't want to miss it. When they finally came on, the lights just barely glowed. I remember my mother smiling. When they came on full, tears started to run down her cheeks.

—Clyde T. Ellis
first general manager of NRECA,
recalling "the night the lights came on"

2

Lights were coming on all over rural America. The first magic glow of the naked bulb was witnessed then—and is recalled today—with a sense of awe.

"The night the lights came on" is often recorded as a high moment in the lives of American rural families: an important date, ranking with marriages and births as a day to cherish. And the recollection of it has become a part of folklore. A Kentucky farmer recalled his boyhood and that memorable event:

"We'd heard the government was going to lend us money to get lights, but we didn't believe it until we saw the men putting up the

3

poles. Every day they came closer, and we realized it really was going to happen. So Dad went ahead and had the house wired.

"It was almost two months later before they finished the job and turned on the power. I'll never forget the day—it was late on a November afternoon, just before dark. All we had was wires hanging down from the ceiling in every room, with bare bulbs on the end. Dad turned on the one in the kitchen first, and he just stood there, holding on to the pull-chain. He said to me, 'Carl, come here and hang on to this so I can turn on the light in the sitting room.'

"I knew he didn't have to do that and I told him to stop holding it, that it would stay on. He finally let go, and then looked kind of foolish."

It was like that all across the land.

Farmers and their families were grateful. They wrote letters of thanks to REA, to President Roosevelt, later to President Truman, telling how rural life and work, living itself, were so much better. At least a dozen letters told of how, when the REA power first lighted their farm kitchen, the farmer or his wife hurled a kerosene lamp out the window. It was common for each member of the family to go through the house, turning on every light, every appliance.

In a small farmhouse in Missouri, a woman ignored the lamps which suddenly burst into brilliance, and ran instead to the kitchen, where her new refrigerator had stood for a month awaiting the current. When she saw that the little light inside really came on, she burst into tears of relief.

One woman, 103 years old, wrote REA to thank the government. She had never felt that she had been born too soon, she said, until the night the lights came. Now she regretted that she would see so little of the future.

All across rural America, families bragged, "We got REA now." That meant they were no longer second-class citizens.

1

2

3

Left: Cooking on an electric range near Florence, Alabama. Below, left: Mrs. Ober Apple was the pleased first consumer of Hancock-Wood Electric Co-operative in Ohio; she was flanked by George Lush, a wiring inspector, and C.C. Doyle, co-op manager. Below, right: This kitchen pump in a Florida home in 1930 was a luxury in its day, but was soon to go the way of the wood stove.

4

5

Opposite page, left: This home at Norris Dam in Tennessee was likely used by TVA as a demonstration of the wonder of an electric kitchen. Opposite page, right: Sketch used by REA in a 1940 publication to portray the value of electricity to the home. Right: The ice man in Harlington, Texas, in 1939 almost looks as if he knew the advent of rural electrification meant his days were numbered.

6

For the homemaker, the most dramatic changes were in the back-breaking work of fueling the wood stove and washing clothes. Right, an electric kitchen in the Tennessee Valley. Middle and lower right: Washday was still an outside affair in the years just after electricity came to rural areas and the tub and washboard discarded—perhaps continued out of force of habit from the days of tending fires and boiling pots. Photos below left showing the improvement of the electric stove over the wood stove are unidentified—the irony, however, is that the upper one was taken in 1931 and the other ten years later.

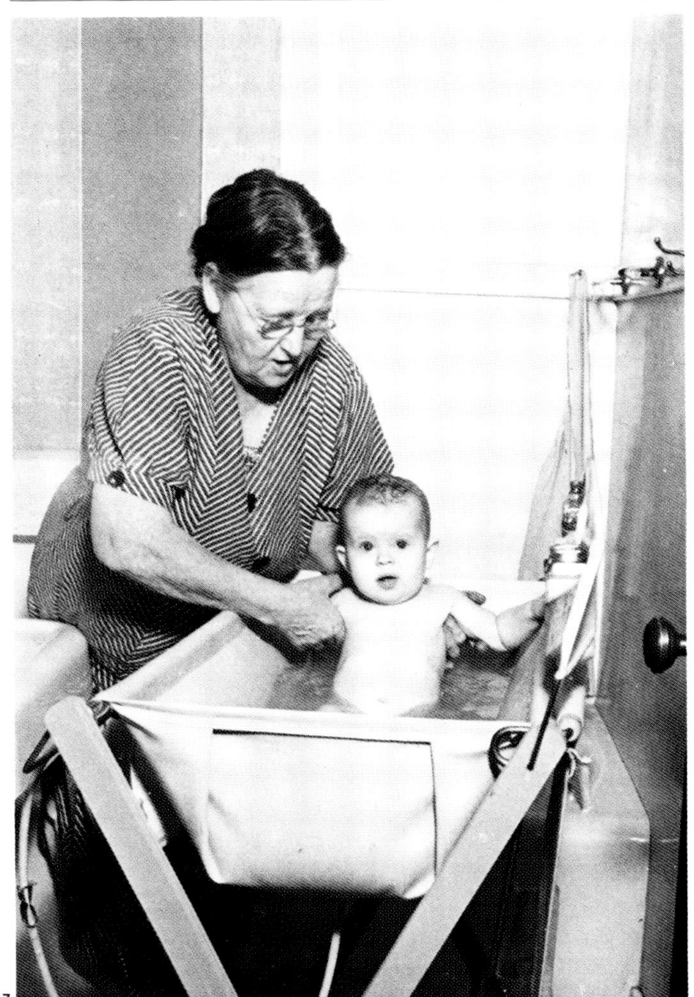
7

8

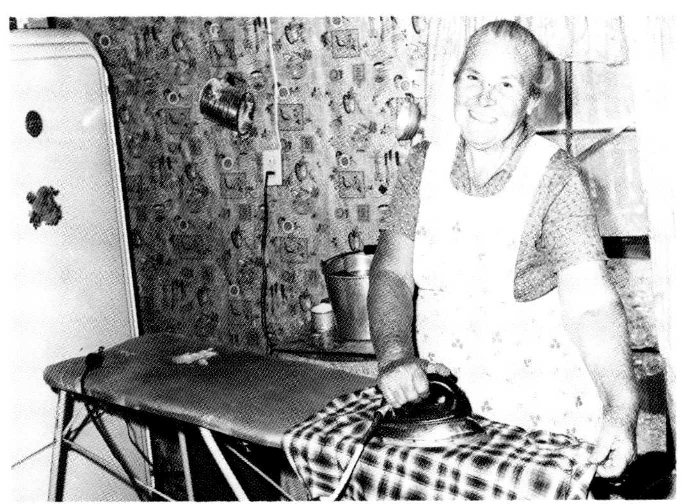
9

10

11

Bathing the baby, ironing, and sewing were other chores made easier by electricity. Top and middle right: Ironing in Arkansas, before and after. Above: Co-op members quickly took on an added task. They learned to read their own meters as a cost-cutting device, as Barbara Keith of Polk County, Missouri, demonstrated.

A Steady 'Hand'

Washing, ironing, cooking, sewing, preserving foods—a hundred household tasks—were revolutionized for the farm wife. And having the blessed light at night changed the way the entire family lived.

At the same time, the men and boys were trying electricity out in the barn. A dairy farmer in Michigan, who milked 50 cows and who had been paying $45 a month for ice, swore by the co-op power. He invested $350 in a milk cooler. Not only did it do a better job cooling than the ice, but the electric bill was only $10 a month!

But the farmer was most taken with the electric motor. Only thing was, he couldn't talk to it. But neither did it give him any back talk.

His idea of a good hired hand was a "steady worker"—one who was healthy and didn't loaf on the job, didn't go off on a periodic spree or wander off in the middle of harvest.

Now he had that steady hand. A one-horsepower motor, the farmer soon learned, could do as much work in an hour as a man could do in a day. It took little attention and needed no prodding or coaxing. It was light and portable and it stayed on the job as long as you wanted it to.

The farmer was quick to use the motor for pumping water and sawing wood. In time, he learned to use electricity to lift hay to the loft and to blow ensilage into the silo. He used it to grind and mix feed and to move feed to the cattle. His wife learned to use it to brood chicks and to increase egg production.

1

2

3

4

REA not only provided assistance to its rural electric borrowers, it tried to help co-op members directly. Upper left: This seed separator was built with plans provided by REA; motor had portable mount so it could be moved for other tasks. Upper right: This corn sheller, on the farm of C.H. Eblin in Bedford County, Tennessee, was operated by a quarter-horsepower electric motor. Right: Bright lights helped a bit as Nona Schwartzbeck began the 4 a.m. chore of getting milk to the calves on her Maryland farm. Opposite page, left: A portable electric motor made the chores of Julien H. Case easier on his Lauderdale County, Alabama, farm in 1942. Opposite page, right: REA used this illustration in a 1940 publication to tell co-op members what a kilowatt-hour of electricity meant to them.

5

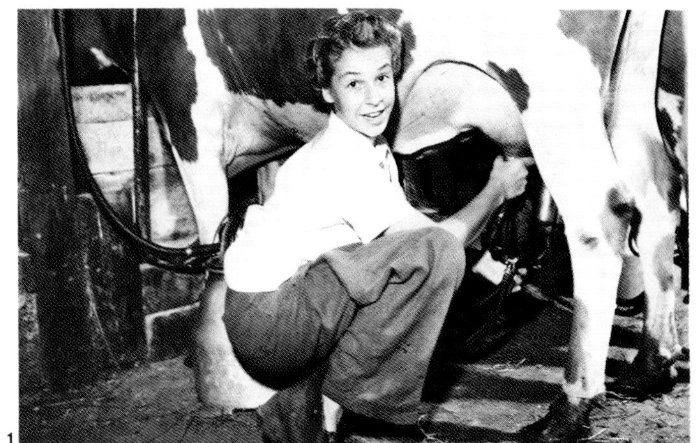
1

2

3

4

5

Upper left: Patricia Doremire using an electric milking machine at her family's farm near Monticello, Indiana; photo was used by REA to tell the story of increased farm production in 1946. Upper right, a Batavia, New York, dairyman kept his milk cool and fresh. Middle left: Milking time in the days before electricity. Middle right: An unidentified 1930s demonstration of a new electric sheep-shearer. Left: Vernon Electric Cooperative member Eddie Saugstad and Manager "Lefty" Leifer (right), checking out electric fence equipment at the co-op offices, Westby, Wisconsin, 1942.

6

Not only did electricity provide the farm family with a servant to help shear the sheep or milk the cows, it meant new business for the town merchant and better quality food for the consumer. And electric brooders and egg candlers helped the farmer's wife increase the "chicken and egg money." For the kids, this meant a few more dollars for school clothes or a rare treat. Upper photo unidentified, lower one was taken in the Tennessee Valley.

7

'Forty Kilowatt-Hours a Month?'

When co-ops were first organized, directors wondered mightily how they and their neighbors were going to use all the electricity the lines were built to carry. Forty kilowatt-hours a month seemed impossible.

Their apprehensions were short-lived. Within 12 months after one project was energized, a survey showed the following purchases of appliances by co-op members:

Electric irons and radios: 84.3 percent
Washing machines: 63.2 percent
Vacuum cleaners: 48.2 percent
Toasters: 35.5 percent
Electric motors: 27.1 percent
Electric water pumps: 16.2 percent

The electric iron, which barely nudged the radio as the most popular purchase, was usually the first item to be brought home. But washing machines, stoves and refrigerators quickly followed.

In community after community, appliance stores flourished as families rushed to join the 20th century.

The promoters and pushers of rural electrification were amazed. The skeptics and critics were confounded.

Opposite page: Unloading a new stove and washing machine at the R.H. Bacon farm in Hamilton County, Tennessee. Right: Eddie Saugstad looking at a Co-op brand washing machine with Manager "Lefty" Leifer at Vernon Electric Cooperative in Westby, Wisconsin. Below left: Co-op members examining an REA "lighting package" at Clyde Borkey's appliance store in Bowling Green, Virginia. Center right: A deliveryman from the Borkey store bringing a new electric refrigerator to the farm home of the Quarles family near Carmel, Virginia, in this photo from early REA files. Bottom right: Deliveryman loading part of lighting package destined for the Quarles place, an REA "exhibit electrified farm."

2

3

4

5

'Return With Us Now to Those Thrilling Days of Yesteryear . . .'

When rural people referred to "The Radio," wrote essayist E. B. White, they meant "a pervading and somewhat godlike presence which has come into their lives and homes."

"The day we got our radio," wrote one farm wife, "we put it in the kitchen window, aimed it out at the fields, and turned it on full blast. During the first week, the men hated to be out of the sound of it."

Without doubt, the radio was the most desired and the most influential of all of the wondrous new appliances that came to the country with rural electrification.

"As soon as we got Momma an electric iron, we got a radio," was often heard. Indeed, the iron barely nudged out the radio as the most popular purchase. In home after home, Crosleys or Philcos became not only a center of information and entertainment but a place to proudly display family photos or other mementos.

REA recognized the potential as early as 1936, noting that "the city dweller looks upon radio solely as a means of entertainment; the farmer relies upon it for the betterment of his economic status as well."

Education by radio would also be important, said the agency, and suggested that "the power lines along the highway should pause at these little schoolhouses to deliver the few watts which stand between the child and the great world in which some day he may be a very important part."

Only two years later, REA reported a remarkable statistic: A survey of co-ops found that 86 percent of their members had a radio—even though the average project had been operating only eight months!

Radio had special meaning for the farm family. Market and weather reports rapidly made it a necessity. Its impact as an educational tool was, said REA, "well-nigh incalculable." The networks, the land-grant universities, the "clear channel" and local stations flooded the airwaves with practical farming advice, market news and—for the homemaker—information on clothes, diet, child psychology, cooking.

1

2

3

4

5

6

Radio was more than entertainment for rural families—it brought them farm, weather and market news and it ended their isolation from world events. Opposite, lower right: Photo of a Swedish-American family from a collection on President Roosevelt's "Fireside Chats." Top, this page: A family listening to news of the European war, about 1940.

7

1

2

3

4

Radio's impact as an educational tool was "well-nigh incalculable," said REA, and children listened (and watched) and learned. "I am a crippled boy of 16 who has a hard time walking about. Our well is 200 feet away from our home and I have to climb a little hill to bring water to the house. My mother can't carry water because she is very sick. If we had the electric we could have an electric pump put in our house," one lad wrote President Roosevelt. But he wanted more than a pump: "It would be nice to have the electric so we could use our radio to listen to your speeches and listen to news of the world and our country." Radio also brought adventure—as Bob Artley remembers (right). Opposite page, bottom: Jerry and Linda Beasley listening to the radio in this REA photo which also pointed out the value of an electric fan. Opposite, top left: Unidentified photo from REA files. Opposite, top right: Home of Robert McWhorter, Woodville, Georgia.

5

6

12:45 pm-1:00 pm - MONDAY Thru SATURDAY

WDAY RADIO - 970 Fargo, N. D.

KFYR RADIO - 550 Bismarck, N. D.

Sponsored By This Local Co-op and The Farmers' Union Central Exchange, Inc.

1

2

3

*The "Co-op Shoppers" (above) entertained Dakota and Minnesota farm families over WDAY and KFYR from the early '40s into the 1960s. Combo members (back, from left): Warren (Dutchy) Gerrells, Don (Azel) Wardwell, Dorothy (Linda Lou) Fandrich, Les (Shorty) Estenson, and (front) Joseph (Little Joe) Stamness, Harry (*what, no nickname?*) Jennings. Show was sponsored by the Farmers Union Central Exchange Monday through Saturday (upper left).*

Above: Everett Mitchell (standing) and Ken Gapen of the National Farm and Home Hour. Right: U.S. Department of Agriculture employees assembled in 1920 to listen to what is believed to have been the first broadcast of market news over an experimental government station.

4

5

Above: Fay Crusch, former Montana NRECA director, brought farm news to eastern Montana and western North Dakota. Right: Frank E. Mullen was first full-time farm broadcaster at KDKA in Pittsburgh, beginning in 1923. Below: WHO, Des Moines, Iowa, a premier farm station, promoted with events such as this "Tall Corn Contest."

6

7

1

2

3

4

5

6

The thirst for knowledge, and the desire to keep up with their city cousins, made rural families an important audience. Almost every conceivable subject was offered over the airways. REA reported that even typing had been successfully taught by radio.

The longest-running program in the history of network radio became "The National Farm and Home Hour." It was on the air daily from October of 1928 to June of 1944 and was a weekly program for a time thereafter. Almost every rural American knew the voice of announcer Everett Mitchell and his daily greeting, "It's a bea-*u*-ti-ful day in Chicago. . . ."

Rural families also listened to the same programs as everyone else.

Sunday nights they gathered around to "watch"—they invariably looked at the radio while they listened to it—Jack Benny, Fred Allen, and Edgar Bergen and Charlie McCarthy. The women followed "Oxydol's own Ma Perkins" and the other soaps. On Saturday night it was the Grand Ole Opry with Red Foley and Minnie Pearl or the National Barn Dance with Lulu Belle and Scotty.

Boys raced home from school to try to finish their chores before the afternoon adventure serials. Rural mothers, as did city mothers, despaired of getting the children to the dinner table on those evenings when the announcer asked them to "return with us now to those thrilling days of yesteryear" while "the Lone Ranger rides again!"

Above all, though, they cherished the opportunity to listen to FDR's Fireside Chats. They had been given the chance to be a part of the political as well as the social life of the day.

When television began reaching rural areas nearly two decades later, it crept in slowly and without the immense impact of radio.

Opposite page, upper left: Two of radio's great comedians, Jack Benny and Fred Allen, trading insults in a 1936 NBC broadcast. Upper right: "Ma Perkins," played by Virginia Payne, was still solving other people's problems when she delivered this 6,027th broadcast July 31, 1957, by then in her 25th year. Other radio immortals were heroic, goofy, terrifying or just marvelous entertainers. At bottom, from left: "Who was that masked man?"—this movie-TV Lone Ranger may or may not have been his voice on early radio; Edgar Bergen in 1942 manipulating the vocal cords of his two sidekicks, Charlie McCarthy and Mortimer Snerd; Orson Welles directing the "War of the Worlds" on Halloween in 1938—with such realism that it caused panic in many areas of the nation; Red Foley, a mainstay of the "Grand Ole Opry," shown here in 1957.

Besides entertainment, rural people sought information and, above all, they wanted to hear FDR's "Fireside Chats." At right, the President just prior to Chat No. 6, September 30, 1934.

7

Bringing Power to the People

From the start, REA realized the importance of educating cooperative consumers about electricity and its uses. The agency set out to do it in a way that was typical of its early activist style.

It took rural electrification on the road with a circus tent and trucks loaded with demonstration equipment for farm and home. This "Farm Equipment Tour" soon became known simply as "the REA circus."

Begun as an experiment in October of 1938, the circus started out in eastern Iowa in a year that saw a bountiful corn harvest. The show made 12 two-day stops across Iowa and ten in Nebraska, ending in western Nebraska just before Christmas.

In 1939, 1940, and 1941, it toured 26 other states, demonstrating, educating and promoting.

It was successful beyond its most ardent supporters' fondest dreams.

Farmers and their families flocked to the circus by the thousands, eager to learn more about electricity and the many labor-saving tasks it could perform.

Word of the circus' success soon reached dealers and manufacturers and they quickly became part of the caravan. Twelve or 14 of them were usually in train with REA and would surround the "big top" with their wares.

They were astounded at how farmers "took" to electricity and how willing (and able) they were to pay for it and for equipment to use it.

Often, when a farmer saw how easily the equipment could be operated, he would become so "sold" that he'd "buy on the spot."

Dealers and "reps" were constantly wiring ahead to arrange for more equipment to be delivered at the next stop.

Many farmers later said the hours spent at the circus often marked a turning point for them. The knowledge gained and the purchasing decisions made "then and there" dramatically changed their farming operations.

And wherever the circus toured, rural electric managers and project superintendents were ecstatic. Memberships grew. Appliance sales skyrocketed. Kilowatt-hour sales showed healthy increases.

Before the REA "big top" folded in late 1941 because of World War II, it had brought its electrifying message to one million farmers.

REA had truly brought power to the people.

1

2

3

The REA circus drew huge crowds to its "big top" (above). What seemed to be a festival-like affair to the curious farm family entering the midway had actually been planned with precision scheduling. REA utilization specialists and home economists relied heavily on local co-op people to make advance preparations and promote attendance (left, above). Women's groups ran cook tents with the latest electric appliances brought to the show by the amazing REA home economists who proved equal, and more, to the grueling circus schedule.

The afternoon of opening day, REA utilization specialists gave lectures and demonstrations on lighting and wiring. Husbands came along with wives, sat on hard benches for hours to watch and learn from the REA home economists. Right: Louisan Mamer, one of the first of the circus crews, giving a home lighting demonstration. Middle right: The circus sparked such intense interest among the farm women that REA had to set up an information booth to distribute printed information. Below: War clouds caused REA to shut down its enormously successful show in 1941. By then the agency had toured 26 states and introduced new and more efficient electrical uses to nearly a million rural people.

4

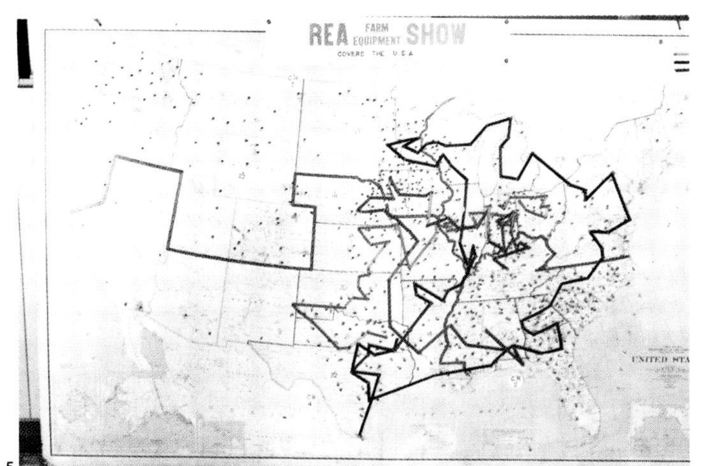

5

6

REA's Dan Teare (right), "ringmaster" of the circus, demonstrating how to construct homemade electric equipment as materials-short war years neared. Home Economist Thelma Wilson extolling features and economies of the electric roaster (below), popular not only with farm wives faced with feeding a score of hired hands, but also a hit for church dinners.

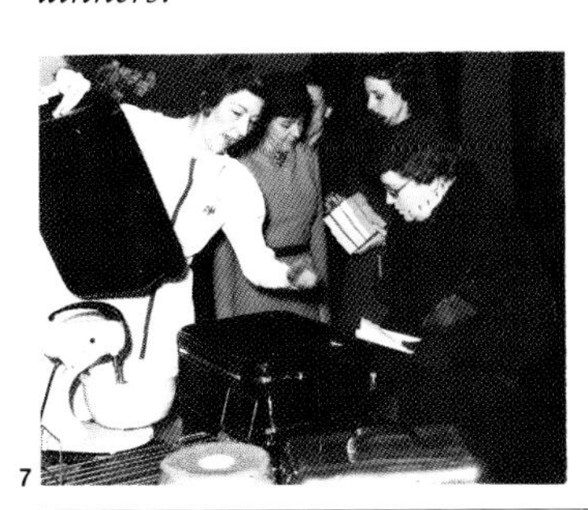

7

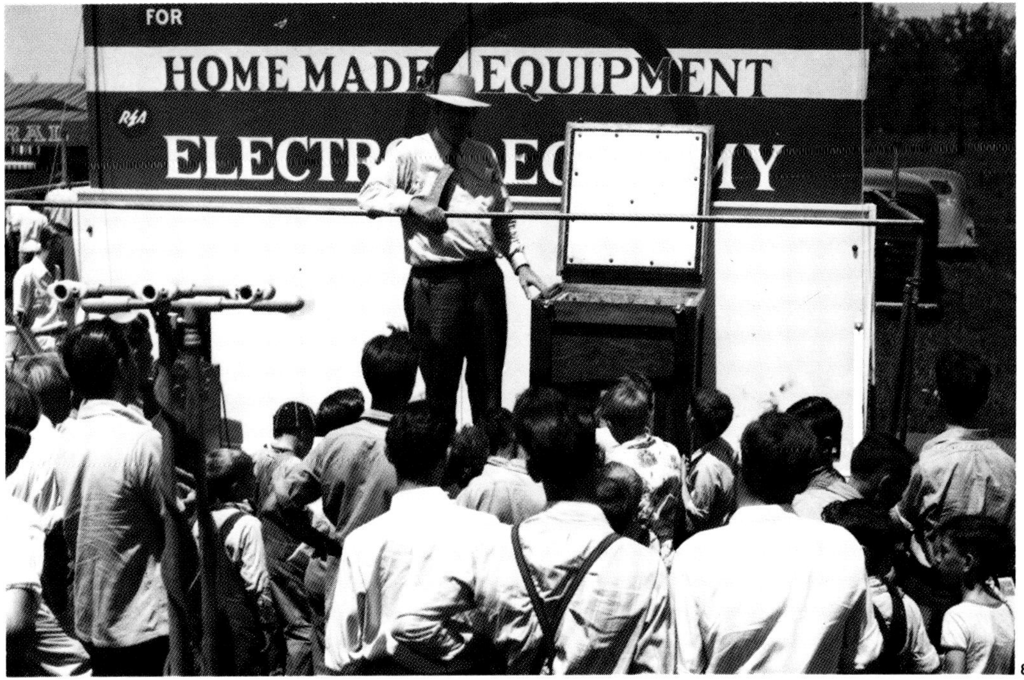

8

1

2

3

4

5

Top: As these 1953 photos show, teaching of farm wiring and plumbing became commonplace in high school vocational agriculture courses after the advent of rural electrification. Middle: REA urged borrowers to run lines to rural schools and the results were dramatic; photo at left is of Oakdale School near Loyston, Tennessee, in October, 1933; at right, an unidentified teacher turning on the lights for the first time in a rural school—to the delight of the children. Left: Late 1930s shot of lines being strung to schoolhouse.

Rural churches not only welcomed electricity but many were important in the formation of electric cooperatives. Such was the case with Mount Paron Primitive Baptist Church, Homer, Louisiana. Its pastor, "Preacher" Brown (the Rev. Andrew E. Brown), was a leader in building his co-op. The photo at right, taken in October, 1945, shows him in the pulpit of his newly electrified church. Below, right: A rural church at Grafton, New Hampshire, without electricity in March, 1941.

6

7

8

Not Just 'Farm Electrification'

It became clear quickly and dramatically why the "program" was "rural" electrification and not just "farm" electrification. It changed everything it touched out there.

"To my mind, the coming of electricity began a new kind of life for most of us," a South Carolina schoolteacher related. "It meant much more than gadgets and appliances. Tenant children used to quit school in the third grade. Now they go through high school, and many finish college. It all happened after the lines came through."

She remembered a tragic grade-school fire which took at least 100 lives in 1926. It began when a child knocked over a kerosene lamp.

The replacement of the coal-oil lamp with electricity changed rural education. It also changed many other facets of rural life. Rural people were now offered respect, equality of opportunity with city people. For one thing, community institutions—churches, schools, meeting and lodge halls—could be used at night.

The pastor of a church at Glidden, Iowa, wrote REA at Christmastime, 1940: "For three years now we have had electric services and now we can hold evening services at any time. Yes, REA has been a boon to our church, as it will be to every rural church located near the lines."

The pastor was quick to add, proudly, that he was vice president of the board of directors of his local co-op.

Crossroads communities, byway places of charm and peace, could now have the additional attractiveness of light and power brought to them by rural electric cooperatives. The lights came to these tiny main streets all over rural America in the late 1930s—places like Bridgeport, Wisconsin (above). The warm and comfortable glow from the little mountain town of Lone Dot ablaze with lights in this painting (left) symbolizes much of what rural electrification and REA meant—and means still—to rural people.

Before the coming of co-ops, the small communities of rural America shut their doors when the sun went down. Now motorists would see the lights up ahead, stop, and bring new business to the small country stores and shops. W.W. Morisette's general store (opposite page) at Camden, North Carolina, was one of the thousands which benefitted in many ways from the coming of the rural light and power.

Electricity Comes to the Crossroads

The crossroads community—a remote cluster of homes with a country store, a filling station, and maybe a school and a church—was transformed by electricity.

The heart of the crossroads, the country store, was still the rural institution it had always been, still the place where the farmer and his wife could buy anything from a box of tacks or a paper of pins to a new mowing machine. But now the store's interior was brightly lighted and customers came evenings, stayed longer.

The wares offered soon included light bulbs, lamps, radios, electric chick brooders, sometimes large kitchen appliances. And there were electrically cooled ice cream and cold drink cabinets, refrigerated meat and produce display cases.

The crossroads also often became the site of a new business—the electric locker plant. In many cases these were financed by REA as a co-op business run by the farmers who now had a way to preserve the foods they raised.

An electric co-op in Wisconsin reported to REA in 1939 that it was serving 15 small country stores, a creamery and mill in a small crossroads town, five garages, three taverns, two pool halls, a blacksmith shop, a tourist lodge, an airfield and a radio beam. "Next is the Boy Scout Camp," the manager wrote REA.

A general store owner in Texas raved about how business was booming since he got the hookup. He had wired "everything I could think of," he told the co-op, including "two big floodlights in front of the store and lights on the gas pumps, too. Tourists used to whiz right by my pumps, but do I have the night business now! They see the lights up ahead and stop. The lights have doubled my gas business."

Another general store operator boasted proudly of his new electric light for a month after he got service—then discovered it was only the night-light over his cash register. When a co-op employee showed him how to turn on the rest of the lights, he was speechless with amazement.

3

Crossroads communities were social centers for rural people. Meeting halls were often makeshift affairs like this potato storage house (above), with seats improvised out of planks and potato crates. The coming of electricity now made night meetings possible. But it was the country store that was the heart of Crossroads America. Merchants expanded their lines and wares, and with refrigeration, offered a wider variety of foods (left). Refrigeration also made possible community meat and frozen food lockers, as L.A. Moon of Etowah County, Alabama (in overalls, opposite page, left), was happy to discover. Co-ops in some instances were able to serve communities the next size up—towns like Shelby, Montana (opposite, top), which got electricity for street lighting from Marias River Electric Co-op. The color, the charm, the appeal were all still there, but electricity gave crossroads main streets and stores, such as this one in North Carolina (opposite, right), a new lease on life.

3

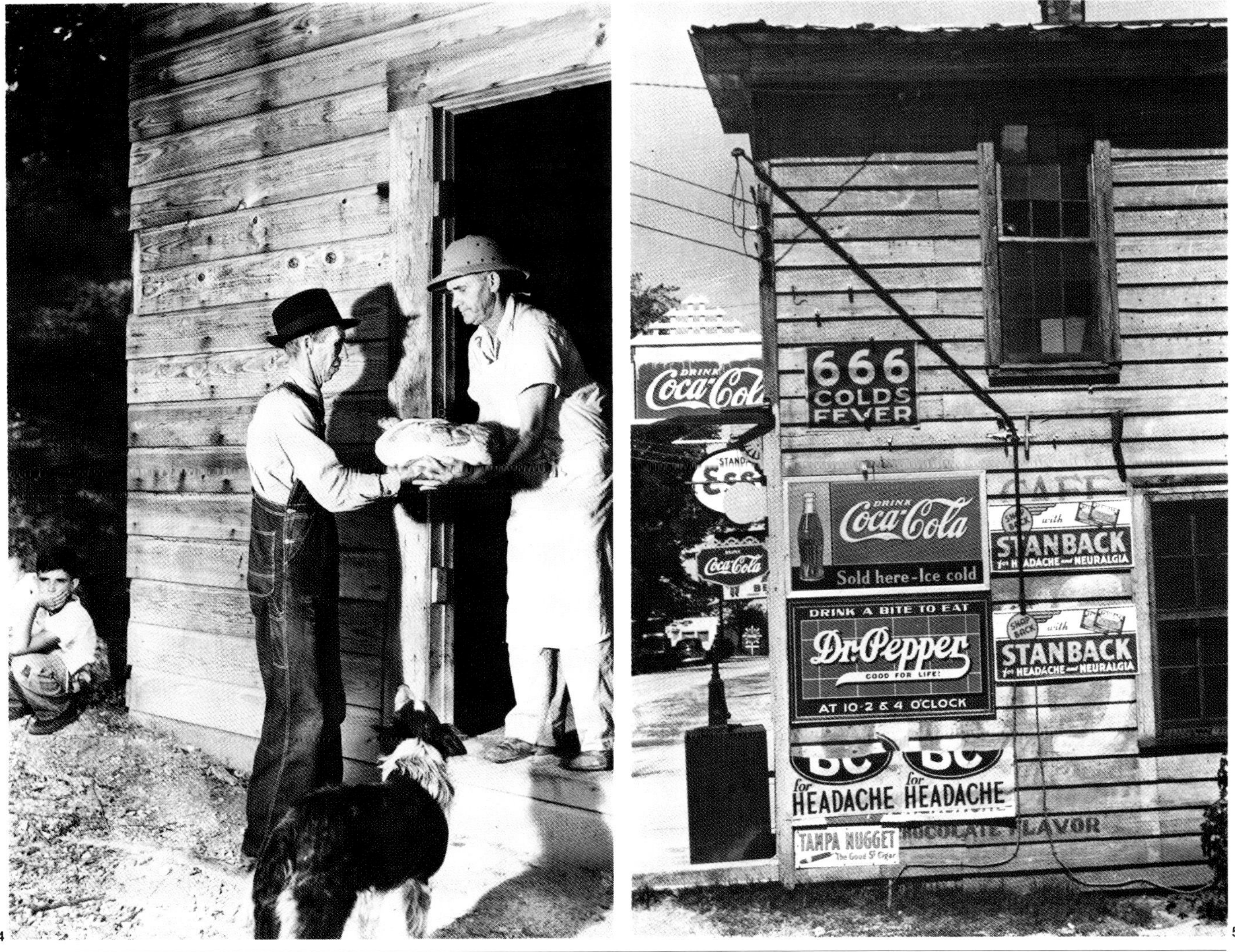
666
COLDS
FEVER
DRINK
Coca-Cola
Sold here-Ice cold
STANBACK
for HEADACHE and NEURALGIA
DRINK A BITE TO EAT
Dr Pepper
GOOD FOR LIFE!
AT 10-2 & 4 O'CLOCK
STANBACK
for HEADACHE and NEURALGIA
BC
for
HEADACHE
BC
for
HEADACHE
TAMPA NUGGET
The Good 5¢ Cigar

4

5

Above: "Preacher" Gloria Allender delivered the funeral oration on June 16, 1938, as a gleaming kerosene lamp was buried and lines of Blue Grass Rural Electric Cooperative, Nicholasville, Kentucky, were energized. The "funeral" was carried out by members of area 4-H clubs. Several formed a chorus which sang "Let the Lower Lights Be Burning" as the casket was lowered. Left: After raising the first pole of Henderson County Rural Electrification Association, a troop of Boy Scouts raised the flag at Henderson, Kentucky. The troop's bugler played taps at the demise of the sooty kerosene lamp. Kentucky's rural electric people, in staging these mock funerals, set a humorous tone that many new co-ops repeated across rural America. Opposite page, right: David Brown, president of Ostego Electric Co-op, Hartwick, New York, pulling the switch energizing the new system's power lines for the first time in June, 1944.

'Rest in Peace'

At a crossroads community in Texas, the night the lines were energized, ranchers filed past a newly dug "grave," throwing their kerosene lamps into the pit as sign of their deliverance.

At graveside services in Pennsylvania, the REA project coordinator solemnly read the "obituary of the oil lamp." As he read, an old kerosene lamp in a paper box coffin was buried. A tombstone was set over the spot.

At ceremonies near Nicholasville, Kentucky, a funeral sermon was preached as four pallbearers lowered into the ground a kerosene lamp. The choir sang, "Brighten the Corner Where You Are." The "mourners" cheered vigorously.

The *Reader's Digest* ran the obituary of this lamp burial by the Blue Grass Rural Electric Cooperative. At that 1938 ceremony, the casket was opened to permit a last look at the "body" which had been polished until "it almost blinded the 'mourners.'" Following the eulogy, climaxed by a parody on a poem by Alfred Lord Tennyson, the chorus sang "Let the Lower Lights Be Burning" as the casket was lowered.

From June of 1936, well into the 1940s, ceremonies such as these took place as the energization of local co-ops swept across the land.

Not all were tongue-in-cheek. Plenty of them had lots of serious words; but the sense of joy, of high moment and great accomplishment was always there. Emotions could not be hidden.

A Vermont co-op invited REA officials to throw the switch which would send current through its new lines. When the moment came, the REA representatives declined the honor, choosing to honor a local leader. Without warning, they called on the woman who had been the "co-op sparkplug." She came proudly to the platform, reached for the switch—and broke into tears. She had to have help to complete the ceremony. Many hands joined hers to press the switch home.

3

4

Right: Ceremonies often attracted local and national politicians: U.S. Sen. Hugh A. Butler (center, in topcoat) at setting of the first pole of Twin Valleys Electric Association, Cambridge, Nebraska. Participants (from left) were Vice President George Mousel; Treasurer Harry E. Smith; Charles Meyerle, director; Sen. Butler; Harry Williams, director; Manager Omar F. Ford. Below: Superintendent Ed Kann read the funeral oration at Adams Electric Cooperative's energization, May 4, 1941.

Hancock-Wood Electric Cooperative, North Baltimore, Ohio, chose a more solemn approach. On December 9, 1938, the co-op (then called Wood-Hancock) staged a ceremony (right) to start line construction on the Edna Clark farm in Liberty Township. J.E. Shoop, president (kneeling, left), held the first stake. Manager C.C. Doyle drove it home. Standing, left to right were directors and other officials: Trontous Amos, Emery Jimison, Carl Hamlin, Victor Sink, G.W. Dick, V.C. Miller and A.S. Piffer.

6

Contractors (left) set first pole of Sheridan REA in Wyoming, September, 1947. Little Nelda Pitsch (below), assisted by father and Sheridan board member Alex Pitsch, broke champagne on pole. "Railbirds" who took in the pole-raising included Pitsch (far left), George Williams, Sheridan director (third from left), Director Walter Elm (in dark shirt), Sheridan board attorney Phil Garbut and William Holland, mayor of Buffalo, Wyoming.

7

8

9

In one of the earliest ceremonies, REA Administrator Morris L. Cooke, left (in familiar black bowler hat), stood ready to commence spadework to plant the first pole for Boone County Rural Electric Membership Corporation, Lebanon, Indiana, January 9, 1936. Standing with Cooke to assist was James K. Mason, treasurer, Indiana Farm Bureau Cooperative Association. The farm group was key to getting rural electrification rolling in the state. After the hole was dug, farmers borrowed a pole from the local warehouse of Public Service Company of Indiana and carried it to the site where it was ceremoniously erected.

1

2

Traveling a country road at dusk in the early 1940s, a land buyer for the Tennessee Valley Authority (TVA) came upon the farmer of a newly electrified farm. Sitting on a little knoll overlooking his farm, he gazed down at his house, barn and smokehouse ablaze with light. The TVA man could not help but notice the look of special wonder in the farmer's face, enthralled at the scene below. About a week later the TVA man attended the church to which this farmer belonged. During the service, the farmer got up to express his spiritual condition, giving witness thusly: "Brothers and sisters, I want to tell you this. The greatest thing on earth is to have the love of God in your heart, and the next greatest thing is to have electricity in your house."

3

REA
CO-OP
CO-OP

Main Street Gets a New Business

As each "REA co-op" was organized it needed office space—and finding it in Depression-ridden rural towns was no problem. Most simply moved into a vacant store in town. So it was that Main Street got a new business in hundreds of towns across rural America.

And a new business meant new jobs. Managers, clerks, linemen and others were quickly recruited as the projects grew into reality. There were lines to build, equipment to be bought, consumers to hookup, bills to be sent.

Something else happened. Rural people experienced the luxury of electricity for the first time—and they rushed headlong into the 20th century. They bought irons, radios, refrigerators, stoves, lights, and more.

The new kid on the block brought a new life to the rest of the businesses on Main Street.

Member Eddie Saugstad and his son Teddy leaving the office of Vernon Electric Cooperative in Westby, Wisconsin. This photo was one of many taken of rural electric cooperative people during the summer of 1942 by famed photographer Arthur Rothstein.

1

RURAL ELECTRIFICATION ADMINISTRATION
CO-OPERATIVE SYSTEM
TO ADVANCE THE POSITION OF AGRICULTURE
TO ENRICH THE LIFE OF THE COMMUNITY
TO FREE MEN AND WOMEN FROM THE HEAVY
DRUDGERY OF THE HOME AND FARM
THIS GENERATING PLANT WAS ERECTED
IN COOPERATION WITH THEIR FEDERAL GOVERNMENT
BY FARMERS OF IOWA MINNESOTA AND WISCONSIN
TO WHOM IT BRINGS THE SERVICE OF ELECTRICITY
TRI-STATE POWER CO-OPERATIVE
GENOA WISCONSIN
1940

2

Left: Plaque follows exactly the wording recommended for generating plants by Administrator Carmody; Tri-State later became a part of Dairyland Power. Carmody told REA borrowers he didn't believe in putting people's names on plaques and cornerstones, "especially if the building is cooperatively owned. It doesn't seem democratic." Lower left: Early Pennsylvania co-op office.

The letters "REA" soon became a common sight in small towns across the nation. Above: Neon rendition in co-op window in Michigan. Opposite page: This Pennsylvania storefront office has co-op name in window, REA on doorway. Below: A more modern rendition of REA logo.

3

4

5

REA Co-op: A Sign for the Times

The "storefront office" was the first home for most rural electrics. At first there was little to distinguish it from other vacant or partly used buildings.

Quickly, though, the "REA Co-op" sign became one of the best-known symbols of the '30s, '40s and into the '50s.

Some co-op leaders, anxious to make the identity of their new organizations known, asked REA to develop a standard symbol of identification.

And those who seemed a little too modest about what they were creating could count on a prod from REA.

Returning from a swing around the country touring REA projects in the summer of 1938, Administrator John Carmody scolded these co-ops in an open letter:

"Do you know that today there are over 400 REA projects, spread over 45 states, and that they will serve approximately 400,000 farm families or perhaps 2,000,000 people?

"Yet I visited a lot of REA-financed projects this past summer only to find that usually a passerby would scarcely know there was a co-operative undertaking in the neighborhood. We ought to do more with signs and posters and pole markers. I consider the small expense well-justified from the point of view of management."

The aggressive Carmody, who always "followed through," then ordered REA to send out drawings and designs and suggested uses for the signs and symbols. For generating plants, he arranged for plaques to be struck.

Carmody told the REA borrowers he didn't believe in putting people's names on plaques and cornerstones—"especially if the building is cooperatively owned.

"It doesn't seem democratic."

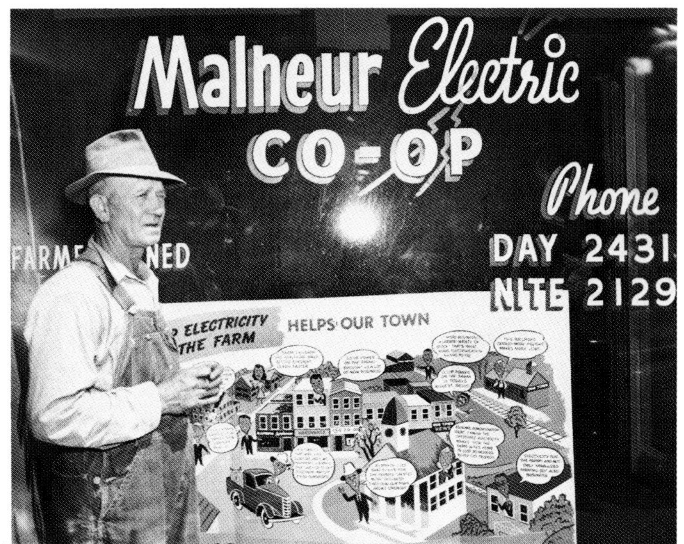

1

2

3

4

Early co-op identifications were seldom uniform, but REA later proposed symbols that were widely used—even in horticultural designs, such as the one above at Burt County Rural Power District in Tekama, Nebraska, 1942.

Right: Virginia sign was the type used to mark earliest rural electric projects. Below: Alabama sign, typical of those which came later.

5

6

7

Local co-ops used REA's sign recommendations, but often added a local touch, as did this Louisiana co-op (right). Above photo may have been taken in Crawford County, Pennsylvania.

8

9

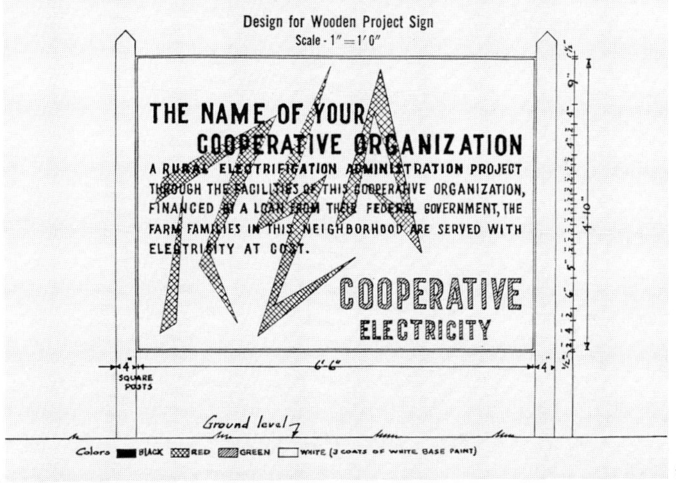

10

In October, 1938, REA proposed standard signs and pole markings for its borrowers (drawings). Photos above and below show the agency's recommendations were taken seriously.

Right: This early home of Rush County (Indiana) Rural Electric Membership Corporation was typical of a co-op in the late 1930s or early 1940s.

11

R
E
A
CO-OP

pole along main highways and about
fifth pole on seco
roads ought to f
bill. We are wo
now on a plan to
it possible to ma
poles at very
cost.

Another spot
can be turned to
account in publi
your story is the
of the project's
or trucks. Perh
series of poster
rying load-buil
suggestions wou
effective. Po
also might go w
the office window or in the windows of
ance dealers. We are working up sor

12

13

Delinquencies on monthly electric bills were rare. Many members would pay their bills six or eight months in advance after the harvest. Paying bills in person remained a habit for many years. Here's a "Saturday" customer (opposite page) in crisp new overalls and tie paying his electric bill at White County Rural Electric Membership Corporation, Monticello, Indiana.

While the manager of a new co-op was heavily involved with contractors' construction crews and co-op linemen out on the system, the bookkeepers were in the front lines at home in the co-op office. It was rare in those years of feverish building that employees were together all in one place. Employees of Hancock-Wood Electric Cooperative (top), North Baltimore, Ohio, got together for the photographer in 1945. Co-ops and their staffs (right, middle left) soon outgrew their first storefront operations. Many of them, like Southside Electric Cooperative, Crewe, Virginia (middle right), later erected modern headquarters (see page 141).

5

The Manager and the Bookkeeper

The manager of an REA project had to run an office, supervise maintenance and construction, plan demonstrations and ceremonies, obtain new members, teach all members ways in which they could use electricity productively, maintain good relations with the membership and the community, carry out the policies of the board of directors and REA, be a good cooperator in spirit and practice, have some knowledge of accounting procedures and understand the capital and operating structure of the cooperative, and be somewhat conversant with the rates and with technical complexities of rural electric lines.

That was a big order, but if some managers were light on any qualifications, they made up for lack of training with hard work and courage.

REA field men in the early years gave a picture of managers or superintendents setting up cots in their offices, cooking with hot plates, living on the job for years. Frequently, they drove their employees hard, field personnel noted, but they often kept the toughest jobs for themselves.

During a storm in Nevada, lightning blew a fuse at the main disconnect switch on a transmission line. A flood that followed washed out the only bridge to the area. So the manager drove more than 200 miles over dangerous mountain roads in the night to replace the fuse. It took him ten hours to do it, but he was on the job in the morning.

The bookkeepers were the other mainstays of the fledgling cooperatives. Their duties were myriad; they definitely did not fulfill the "nose-to-the-ledger" stereotype.

Most often a woman, but not always, the bookkeeper "ran things" while the manager was out on the project, which was a good deal of the time.

The bookkeepers had as many, if not more, direct dealings with the co-op members as the

1

Bookkeepers could always count on their Saturday nights out starting pretty late. Farmers would drop in, pay their monthly bills (left, below right), and visit. The manager was usually around all day, too, available until the eight o'clock closing time to discuss problems with members. He spent more time there weekends than he did all week. In the co-op lobby of Oconto Electric Cooperative, Oconto, Wisconsin, Lineman Henry Kralapp (below left) studied bulletins, noting all the co-op's safety awards.

2

3

manager. They helped develop the cooperative spirit in emphasizing that a promptly paid bill was a payment not only for the electric service but for most of the cost of the member's new line. They helped build electric loads, improving the financial condition of the system. Quite often it was the bookkeeper who suggested to a farm wife that she buy that washing machine, roaster or refrigerator. They often had the job of getting out the co-op newsletter.

A young woman bookkeeper in Georgia quite ably took over the management of her system when the regular manager went off to World War II. The small co-op had lost almost all its help by then and had only one lineman throughout the war, but the "temporary" manager kept the system operating all the same, even rustling up enough materials from an understanding electric supply company to manage construction of ten miles of line.

When the private utility in the area erected "spite-line" poles in the co-op's territory, she organized a confrontation meeting with the utility and co-op officials and the farmers involved. Result: the farmers voted unanimously to "hold out for the REA."

The co-op folks called the young bookkeeper-turned-manager the " 'lectric light lady." During her long, "temporary" tour of duty, she put the system in the "black" for the first time, something the first manager had been unable to do. But he knew he had left the co-op in good hands, because before he left for the war, he married the " 'lectric light lady."

4

Early managers, like Paul Waite (above), Dennys River Electric Co-op, Meddybumps, Maine, operated mostly out of their pickups. Some systems had to "make do," like Golden Valley Electric Association, Fairbanks, Alaska (top right). Doris Olson (at left) and Betty Lou Carpenter took turns stoking the stove. Others like Southside Electric Co-op, Crewe, Virginia (middle right), built modern headquarters following REA architects' designs. Okefenoke REMC's wartime manager was " 'lectric light lady" Mrs. Clara Cox (below). By the 1950s, a modern generation of managers was emerging, typified by Leo T. Callahan (below right), in 1953 the nation's youngest, posing (at left) at Baker Electric Cooperative, Cando, North Dakota, with Glenn Long, office manager.

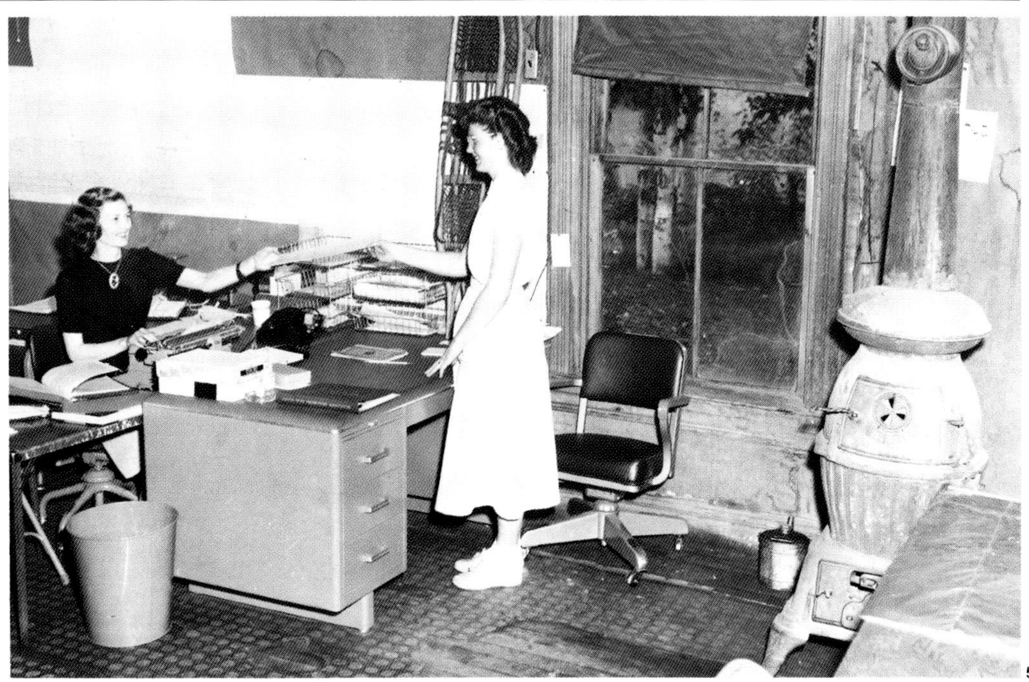
5

6

7

8

'So Here's to the Lineman . . .'

So here's to the lineman, sonofagun!
He'll go without sleep for a week,
Working for you 'til every bit's done,
So the feeders can carry their peak.
Here's to the lineman!

The one co-op employee the rural family came to know—and appreciate—more than all others was the lineman.

He became the co-op's representative out on the land and along the lines. Whether the work was routine or an emergency, members often were on hand with hot coffee and sandwiches or to assist with a stuck truck.

But it was especially during emergencies that the lineman earned the farm family's trust and respect. Co-op linemen's feats of courage and endurance in winter storms, hurricanes, tornados or floods have become commonplace, almost expected.

It isn't just the 20-hour days spent restoring power that have earned respect. Almost always linemen are in the vanguard of those who arrive in the wake of a disaster and they respond to members' needs far beyond restoring power.

Distribution of food, medicine or supplies, helping flood victims dry out their homes with co-op heaters, spotting an accident and responding with life-saving first aid, using the radio to pass on a welcome "we're safe" message—all in a day's work for "the heroic lineman."

1

2

Left: Linemen from Southside Electric Cooperative, Crewe, Virginia, hanging a transformer at the home of the Cabaniss family. Lower left: Co-op member Eddie Saugstad visiting with a lineman for Vernon Electric Cooperative, Westby, Wisconsin, in August, 1942. Photographer Arthur Rothstein focused on Saugstad and his co-op for one of many photo essays on rural electrification. Right: A Newberry Electric Cooperative crew repairing a line in South Carolina. Below: Illinois linemen at work in 1945.

3

4

5

6

Left: Veteran lineman Frank Abanatha of Bossier Rural Electric Cooperative during hurricane Betsy. He and 500 linemen from throughout the South spent days restoring power for members of Louisiana cooperatives in the aftermath of the September, 1965, storm. Above: A definite "no-no"—co-op member Julien H. Case repairing a transformer near his farm in Lauderdale County, Alabama, in June, 1942. Below: The linemen of Clark Rural Electric Cooperative, Winchester, Kentucky.

7

1

On land or water—or on the reservation: Co-op linemen have had a hand in building and maintaining nearly half of all the electric distribution lines in the United States. Left: Clarence Gordon, Frank Jones and Howard Ely loading an "REA standard" pole onto a specially designed truck in Kentucky, probably at Inter-County Rural Electric Cooperative, 1940. Bottom left: Working from a boat, linemen of Clearwater Valley Light and Power Association, Lewiston, Idaho, installed a conductor in 1940 on a line crossing the Grand Canyon of Snake River, the nation's deepest gorge. The line, which carried power across the Snake River to Clearwater Valley members in Asotin County, Washington, was 1.3 miles long and believed to be the longest span of free-swinging electric cable in the U.S. at the time. Below: Showing the tools of the trade in Texas and (bottom) Maryland.

2

3

4

5 6

7

8

Tornados, hurricanes and ice storms are natural disasters that mean long, hard hours of dangerous work for linemen. Top left: A New Mexico ice storm, 1973. Top center: Tornado damage in Mississippi, 1971. Top right: Mark Bonner, manager of the state association of Louisiana electric cooperatives, directing clean-up activities by the light of a kerosene lamp following hurricane Betsy in 1965. Above: An example of Betsy's devastation—the only pole that could be seen in a ten-mile stretch of transmission line of Jefferson Davis Electric Co-op in Cameron Parish, Louisiana. Middle: A Kansas lineman could still smile after storm clean-up. Middle right: Keeping the right-of-way cleared of dead trees is important preventive maintenance. Lower right: Nespelem Valley Electric Co-op employees (from left) Roscoe Olhi, Harry Nanamkin and Harry Butler deciding where to put service pole at home on Colville Indian Reservation in Washington, 1940. Sitting is "sidewalk superintendent" Chuck Jackson.

9

10

11

1

2

3

4

Top: Malheur Electric Cooperative board meeting for the last time May 16, 1949—just before members voted to sell to Idaho Power after ten years of strife. Middle left: Unidentified board stressing importance of member education. Middle right: Middle Tennessee Electric Membership Corporation board in 1945. Bottom: Meeker Cooperative Light and Power board in a Litchfield, Minnesota, courtroom. Opposite right: This 1936 photo of a board meeting of Blue Ridge Electric Membership Corporation, North Carolina, often was used by REA to promote women's participation. From left: James Laxton, Mrs. Fannie Greet, Caldwell County Extension Agent R.O. Carrithers, Mrs. Clyde A. Bowman, R. McCormick Jones.

The Co-ops: Grass-Roots Leadership

Where before there had been no electricity and no chance of ever getting it, the REA loan program gave a glimmer of hope. But it was local leadership and the efforts of the committed few that made it all happen.

These men and women provided what no government agency could. They mobilized grass-roots desires and feelings for electricity into something new and potent: the "membership" of a local rural electric cooperative.

The early organizers most often were elected to the board of directors of the new rural electric system. They had done the talking-up and signing-up, staking their good names and reputations on a successful outcome. Now it was up to them to "make good" on it all. Now that the new electric system was operating, the board was entrusted by the membership to make the right decisions, enabling the system to operate efficiently and economically and on a nonprofit cooperative basis—but with enough revenues for the system to "pay out" and pay back the REA loan.

Tasks facing an early co-op board included retaining legal counsel and directing incorporation and organization . . . electing directors and officers in a manner prescribed by law . . . passing resolutions in conformance with bylaws . . . designing the system through competent engineers . . . arranging for a source of wholesale power at a reasonable rate . . . calculating revenues, costs of construction and operation, and retirement of debt . . . establishing feasibility of "pay out" in devising the new system . . . if not feasible, obtaining more members, redesigning the system. . . . Final feasibility: projecting long-term relationship between revenues, costs and amortization of debt for payment of REA loan, retirement of patronage capital and reserves.

Phew!

5 *Anna Dahl*

6 *Lillian Sears*

7 *Lucy Smith*

8 *Christine Durnin*

Rural electric women who played significant roles as directors, officers and employees over the years include from left, above: Anna Dahl, secretary and later president of Sheridan Electric Cooperative, Medicine Lake, Montana, addressing the 1957 NRECA annual meeting; Mrs. Lillian Sears, "sign-up" veteran of Carroll Electric Cooperative, Berryville, Arkansas, and its president, 1946-1949; "Miss Lucy" Smith, incorporating director, secretary, Lumbee River Electric Membership Corporation, Red Springs, North Carolina; Christine Durnin, early editor for Wisconsin Rural Electric Cooperative Association, later home service advisor, Barron County Electric Cooperative, Barron, Wisconsin.

9

1

Left: "Uncle" John Hobbs addressing the annual meeting of Petit Jean Electric Co-op, Clinton, Arkansas, August 12, 1949. Hobbs came to Arkansas from England in 1886 and in the late 1930s helped organize the co-op. "REA is faith in people," Uncle John said. Below: Members of Northeast Electric Power Association crowding in front of the Ritz Theater, Oxford, Mississippi, for their 1949 annual meeting. They shared billing on the marquee with Virginia Mayo, Eddie Bracken, and another well-known actor.

2

3

Annual meeting sites are as varied as the territories cooperatives serve. Auditoriums, stadiums and tents have been popular choices. In the summer, meetings were often outdoors because of the lack of air conditioning. Even today, with many other diversions clamoring for the attention of co-op members, rural electric annual meetings are often the same "big" attraction they were in the 1930s, '40s and '50s. Right: Manager H.M. Zaricor of Scott-New Madrid-Mississippi Electric Cooperative, Sikeston, Missouri, explaining to members where their 1948 dollars went.

'The Cooperative's the Thing'

Annual meeting day became a high point of the year for many rural families.

The day-to-day activities of the cooperative were carried out by the manager and his staff. The policymakers—the board of directors or trustees—met monthly to give them guidance and direction.

Thus it would go for 364 days of the year. But on the 365th day, under the co-op's bylaws, the members assumed control. Then, assembled in annual meeting, they heard and acted upon the reports of their officers and employees. They elected new directors or reelected incumbents. They made the changes they thought necessary in their bylaws and procedures. And, if all was not well in the co-op, this was the day for them to set matters right.

To be sure, entertainment and prizes spurred attendance, but the idea that the member-owners were indeed just that became firmly implanted in the rural electrification program.

The familiarity of rural people with cooperatives was important, but the role of REA was also instrumental.

When REA Administrator John Carmody made the decision to actively help the new cooperatives learn the electric business, the agency went to work with typical thoroughness.

Not only did it provide assistance with technical and financial matters, but it insisted that members be educated about cooperatives.

Among other programs, by 1945 it had distributed millions of its *Guide for Members of REA Cooperatives*. In a straightforward manner, it stressed the individual member's role and stake in the local rural electric system through a series of questions and answers.

Its answer to the question "Why Go to Annual Meetings?" was blunt:

"Because your REA co-op will never be successful unless you and your fellow-members are active in it. The best board of directors will lose interest and do only a half-hearted job if it knows that the members do not care. A poor board will not do its job properly and you may get poor service and pay too much for it. If members allow that to happen, it will cost them a lot of time and money to get things straightened out. They will also have lost good will and general community support which will be hard to regain."

That kind of advice made "The cooperative's the thing" a lasting byword in rural electrification.

Right: Members waiting in their coats at the annual meeting of Joe Wheeler Electric Co-op in Decatur, Alabama, December 14, 1946. Below left: A record 58 percent of the members of Petit Jean Electric Co-op attended its 1950 annual meeting—2,033 out of 3,509 eligible to vote. Below right: The tent goes up for the annual meeting of Sioux Valley Empire Electric Association, Colman, South Dakota. Temporary seating in the tent accommodates 3,500 for what is one of the largest gatherings of the year in the southeastern part of the state.

1

2

3

4

5

Above: Aerial antics promoting Pioneer Electric Cooperative's annual meeting, Greenville, Alabama, July 9, 1947. Left: Part of the large crowd at a special meeting of Tombigbee Electric Cooperative, Guin, Alabama, October 6, 1950. After "heated" discussions, members voted 655 to 608 not to sell their cooperative to Alabama Power Company.

Right: NRECA's first general manager, Clyde T. Ellis, an inspiring orator and popular speaker at local co-op annual meetings, addressed members of Mississippi County Electric Co-op in Arkansas, September, 1951. At far left in back is Arkansas Gov. Sid McMath. Below: Members of Oakdale Electric Co-op in Wisconsin were among the 1,500 people who gathered to listen to the "Rainbow Rangers" at a live radio broadcast sponsored by Wisconsin electric co-ops.

6

7

Bottom left: Members of Southeastern Michigan REC, Adrian, resoundingly defeated board candidates favoring a sell-out, March, 1949. Below: Member Foster Funk opposing selling to Idaho Power at meeting of Prairie Power Co-op, Fairfield, Idaho, October 7, 1950. His side carried the day. Bottom right: Some 1,300 members of Southern Maryland Electric Cooperative and 2,000 guests registered for the 1958 annual meeting on the lawn of Charlotte Hall Military Academy.

8

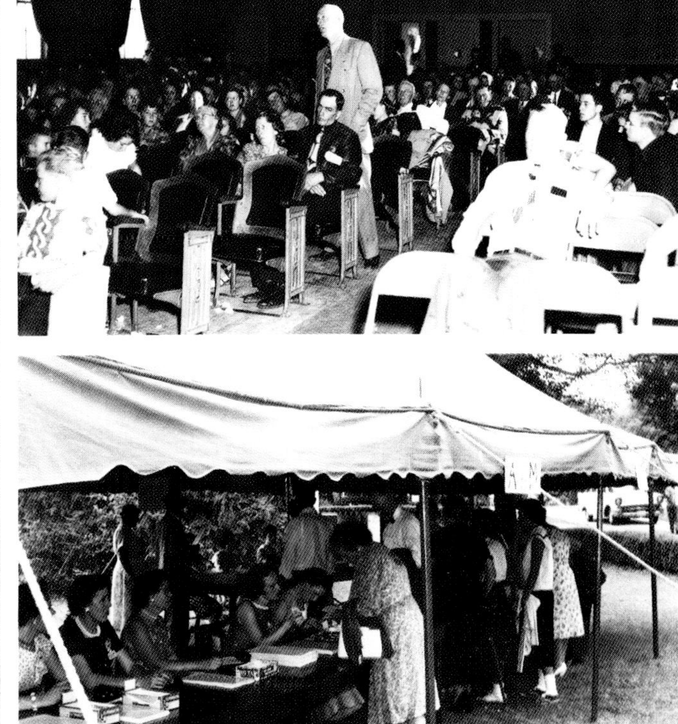

9

10

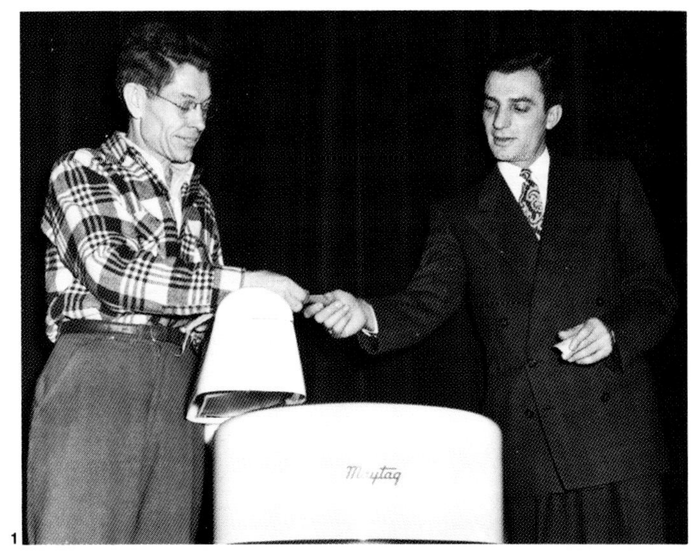

Top left: Eugene Shackleton (at left) drew winning door prize at 1951 meeting of Chugach Electric Association, Anchorage, Alaska, from Chugach employee Anthony Lumbis. Top right: "Tableau of Light" skits were popular out west in late 1930s. Middle left: A few of 400 pies at 1949 annual meeting of Scott-New Madrid-Mississippi Electric. Middle right: Vice President Hubert Humphrey (center) at Eastern Iowa Light & Power Cooperative annual meeting, Wilton Junction, September, 1965. Manager F.E. Fair is at right. Right: Ninnescah Rural Electric Cooperative Association members at Pratt, Kansas, looking over appliances at early 1950s meeting.

6

7

Above: Balloons and prizes drew kids to the 1961 annual meeting of Davie Electric Membership Corporation, Mocksville, North Carolina. Left: At 1956 annual meeting of Southside Electric Cooperative, Crewe, Virginia, Vice Presidential Candidate Estes Kefauver was glad this young tyke couldn't vote. Below left: Elisha Rodgers (at right) won an electric range at the 1948 annual meeting of Pearl River Valley Electric Power Association, Columbia, Mississippi. Master of Ceremonies Kelly J. Hammond told folks all about it. Below right: At 1946 annual meeting of Sand Mountain Electric Cooperative, Fort Payne, Alabama, members viewed appliances.

8

9

1

THE STARS: A real-life REA family, the Bill Parkinsons (left), played themselves in Power and the Land. *Family members (from left) are Father Bill, Mrs. Parkinson (Hazel), Ruth, "Bip" (Frank), Tom and Jake. "We get together and cut the corn," goes the harvest song in the movie. In the scene below left, Bill, Tom and Jake guide the freshly cut corn into a chopper for feed for their dairy cows. Mrs. Parkinson, performing "woman's work, never done" chores (bottom left), darns stocking by light of kerosene lantern. This photo has often been published to depict a woman's lot in the farm home "before electricity." Bottom right: Farmers getting together at Bill Parkinson's place to talk about organizing an electric co-op. The man doing all the talking was an REA field man. Bill Parkinson is standing with hand on pump. Seated next to him was a real-life organizer of Belmont Electric, Hayes Ramsey. This photo has often been used to illustrate co-ops being organized.*

2

3

4

Power and the Land: A 'Real REA Family'

You and me and the neighbors, too—
We get together and cut the corn. . . .

We can get the power and get the light—
We can get the things we want today
With neighbors working the self-same way.
—Stephen Vincent Benet

So went the harvest song in the motion picture, *Power and the Land*, a 30-minute documentary film about cooperative rural electrification. Although not released until November, 1940, the film was shown in more than 1,000 theaters by Christmas.

Power and the Land was produced in the summer and fall of 1939 for REA by the U.S. Film Service. Directed by the noted Dutch filmmaker, Joris Ivens, and filmed in the St. Clairsville area of rural Ohio, the film told a story of what it was like for a rural family to live and work on a farm "before electricity." Then it related how farmers got together and organized an REA co-op, and, finally, how electricity's comforts, economies and easier working methods changed the life of the family movingly and dramatically.

Ivens chose not to use professional actors. Instead, he took the risky course of selecting a "real REA family." That family was the Bill Parkinsons of the nearby Belmont Electric Cooperative. In addition to Bill, the stars were his wife, Hazel, and their five children—Dan, then 23; Tom, 21; Jake, 17; Ruth, 13; and Bip, 8.

In addition to outstanding direction by one of the great artists of documentary films, the Film Service and REA also obtained a distinguished writer-narrator and a noted music composer. The writer and narrator was the acclaimed American poet Stephen Vincent Benet. The composer was Douglas Moore, director of the music department of Columbia University.

Power and the Land had a dual purpose—to publicize and celebrate the successful national program of rural electrification for city audiences and to encourage farmers to continue to organize electric co-ops. The film not only accomplished those purposes, it was acclaimed by critics in the nation's major newspapers and film trade publications as an artistic achievement.

5

Left: Dutch filmmaker Joris Ivens (left) directed the film; Ed Lock was scriptwriter. Right: Cameraman adjusting lens to get full frame for harvest scene. Below: Composer of the film score, Douglas Moore, a noted composer of serious contemporary music, visited the "set" to get the feel of the film and try out the family's piano.

6

7

1

2

3

4

"An REA Production," read the banner premiering Power and the Land *displayed prominently across the main thoroughfare of St. Clairsville (upper left)—scene of several on-location visits by the film crew. The premiere ceremonies led off with the St. Clairsville High School Band performing in blaring good form as it passed the Belmont Co-op offices next to the Old Trail Theater (above). Many filmgoers gathered from town and the surrounding countryside (opposite page). Most had come to see a newly released movie filmed on location in their area. But for some, the day was extra special, giving them cause for possible "premiere jitters." That was because they had roles in the film. Two who did were (bottom left) Hayes Ramsey (center) and Jim Fulton (right), Belmont County Commissioner, visiting with a mere mortal moviegoer from town.*

5

'Symphony In Celluloid' Premieres at Home

For its first showing anywhere, *Power and the Land* was taken back to the "home of the stars" at St. Clairsville, Ohio.

The Parkinsons, the "real REA family," were joined by their neighbors as the Old Trail Theater became the scene of a "world's premiere" on August 31, 1940.

St. Clairsville, Belmont Electric Cooperative, and the townspeople were the honorees that day. Many of them had had "walk-on" or bit parts in the film. The Belmont Electric farmer-directors had played themselves. So had most of the co-op's employees.

A number of local, state and federal officials also attended and messages were read from the governor, the REA administrator and other dignitaries. St. Clairsville Mayor Brady Bradfield declared the day as "REA Day" and the entire county celebrated. As the months went by, similar celebrations were held in other rural towns when the movie opened.

"A superbly photographed and enormously effective statement," said one critic. Another said it was "a symphony in celluloid and as powerful and moving a drama as the cinema capital has ever turned out."

Long since filed away by its distributor, RKO Radio Pictures, *Power and the Land* continues through the years to hold a place of distinction as a "classic" documentary film, often mentioned with such other outstanding creations as *The River* and *The Plow That Broke the Plains*. A film critic recently reviewing it for the National Archives noted that it long ago "transcended its original purpose by providing us with a timeless portrait of American farm life, rich in pastoral beauty and its celebration of traditional American values."

'Not Just Electricity Alone'

While REA had its people in the field to record the "why" and "how" of lighting rural America, another government agency also had photographers abroad. Employed by the Farm Security Administration, these pioneering artists saw the countryside with an indignant eye through a harsh lens and brought the true depths of the Depression to the conscience of the nation. Among them were some of the nation's most famous photographers: Arthur Rothstein, Dorothea Lange, Russell Lee, Jack Delano, John Vachon, John Collier.

Rothstein continued his work with the Office of War Information after 1941. Along the way he recorded the activities of rural people and their electric co-ops in Wisconsin, Iowa and Missouri. At Pemiscot-Dunklin Electric Co-op in Hayti, Missouri, he produced a photo essay of the new system's democratic processes.

1

Now an editor of *Parade* magazine, Rothstein recalled in 1984 his July, 1942, assignment:

"I can shut my eyes and be back in Hayti immediately. There, and everywhere, was a real story to tell. To me, rural electrification was always one of the most important and stirring of the New Deal programs.

"I had spent a great deal of time traveling across the country photographing the conditions. I saw the tremendous hardships farmers and their wives and families had to face. I saw that because they were too distant from the lines they were denied the power and the light.

"And I was so taken with the concept of cooperation as the means by which the government and the people came together to accomplish the rural electrification. . . . It was so in keeping with the magnificent trait in the American character, to knit and band together in times of adversity in order to survive.

"Still, the REA people went beyond survival with cooperative rural electrification. They truly brought and built something to and for themselves. Not just the benefits of electricity alone. . . . They built these co-ops to stand as a statement of what they were capable of achieving under cooperative democratic principles."

2

Photographer Arthur Rothstein (above) went around the offices and lines of Pemiscot-Dunklin in July, 1942, recording the governing and operating processes of the new co-op for the Office of War Information (OWI). He captured the co-op president, Judge T.R. Cole (opposite page, top), as he spoke to neighbors and members about co-op principles as applied to rural electrification; he depicted Manager Glenn Eaker (opposite page, bottom) instructing members and employees on metering of electricity. Left: Eaker briefing members about "where a dollar goes" in co-op revenues to operate the system. Director Avon Knight (front row, far right) later became co-op president.

PEMISCOT-DUNKLIN ELECTRIC COOPERATIVE
Interest and Amortization Schedule
Showing
Total Monthly Debt Service
As Compared To
WHAT A SUCCESSFUL REA CO-OP MEANS
1. Economical service to its members.
2. An asset to the community.
3. Increase in farm and community income.
4. Ownership by the people themselves.
5. Encouragement to do other jobs cooperatively.

3

Meter Watt Hrs = Revolutions x Watt Hr Constant
True Watt Hrs = Stand. Indication X Watt Hr Constant of Standard
Per Cent Accuracy is obtained by ÷
Thus % Accuracy = Meter Watt Hours / True Watt Hours
5 Amp 2 Wire 120 Volt
20 X .6 X 100 / 20 X .6 = 1200 / 12
15 Amp 3 Wire 240 Volt
20 X 3 X 100 / 16.67 X 3.6 = 6000 / 60 = 100%
15 Amp 2 Wire 120 Volt
25 X 1 X 100 / 13.89 X 1.8 = 2500 / 25 = 100%
15 Amp 3 Wire 240 Volt West
25 X 2 X 100 = 5000 / 50 = 100%

4

1

2

3

In July of 1942, most of the cooperative's employees had gone off to World War II, leaving a small nucleus crew to operate the system and erect a few lines in isolated patches of the service area. Opposite page: Foreman Ira Light (upper left) posing with the few remaining reels of copper conductor left on hand. At upper right, Lineman Cecil Sanders, the co-op "troubleshooter," climbing a pole on a routine maintenance assignment. A co-op truck (bottom) operating gear to raise pole on a lucky member's farm (workmen unidentified). Right: Troubleshooter Sanders checking voltage at a co-op substation. Lower left: Lineman Milton Kelley, who later got into the electrical contracting business, in rear of truck at substation. Lower right: Unidentified manufacturer's representative testing and mounting meters which await war's end to be installed. When the co-op's employees returned after the war to take up the task of extending rural electric service to all the members, Pemiscot-Dunklin by the early 1950s became the largest rural electric distribution system in Missouri. Extension of lines to all of this cooperative's members became possible after 1945 because Congress liberalized REA interest rates and loan terms, making "area coverage"—electricity for all—a reality.

4

5

6

1

2

THE MEMBERSHIP: Pemiscot-Dunklin people (opposite page and above) posing outside their co-op's storefront office on South Third Street, Hayti. Rothstein's artistry recorded the sense of community and co-op pride each member shared. In photo at left, hatless man with tie (center) is co-op board director Dave Andrews. At right, Judge Cole, board president, discusses meter reading at his farm with Lineman Sanders. The present manager, David H. Wilkerson, who first came to Pemiscot-Dunklin as a young man in 1938, says of the membership, then and today: "Our people have always been close to the co-op. They understood why they couldn't all get power at first and were patient even after the war years. We work things out together. And, would you believe, that after 48 years, we still have not ever had to pay one dime for a right-of-way easement across a member's land?"

3

1

2

3

4

5

6

When OWI Photographer Arthur Rothstein arrived in Missouri on his mid-west tour of rural electric cooperatives, he was accompanied to the Pemiscot-Dunklin Cooperative by REA photographer Estelle Campbell. She took that opportunity to photograph a series of character studies of its member-owners. Campbell's subjects shown here (opposite page and above) sat for the portraits just prior to voting for directors at the co-op annual meeting. Several of the portrait subjects are in the group photo by Campbell at right. As effectively as Rothstein revealed aspects of Pemiscot-Dunklin's governing and operating life, Campbell composed these portraits to emphasize the human qualities of the rural electric co-op's members: Intelligence and strength, determination and purpose, pride in their new enterprise.

7

Pearl Harbor and America's entry into World War II brought a halt to the advancing REA lines as the agency's role shifted to accelerated wartime food production—powered by electricity. Above: REA's wartime plaque recognizing outstanding agricultural production. Right: Women assembling bomber aircraft hull in defense plant. Left: U.S. battleship West Virginia explodes from direct hit by Japanese bomber, Pearl Harbor, December 7, 1941.

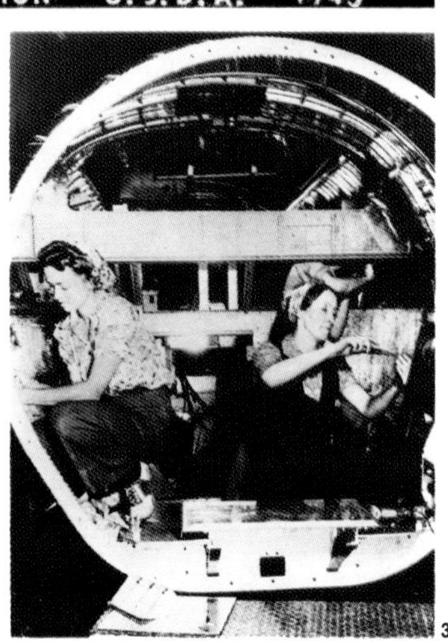

Nearly 200 staff people had left REA for the armed services by December, 1942. Many dropped by REA to visit and be wished well before heading overseas. Among these were Army Lt. Harold W. Kelley (bottom left); Navy Yeoman Russell Goodwin (above left) and Women's Army Corps Private Zelda Krinowitz (above). Right: REA promoted wartime food production in Rural Electrification News.

THEY'RE EATING WELL

And it's the food you're raising that is going on their plates, and on the plates of millions of young men and women like them in the armed forces of our own country, and of our allies.

That's the main thing . . . that our folks in the services eat the right food, and enough of it. Their continued strength and health will help to bring them back sooner—and your food will have had a part in it.

RURAL ELECTRIFICATION ADMINISTRATION, U. S. DEPARTMENT OF AGRICULTURE

From 1935 until early 1941, REA's base was Washington's Westinghouse mansion (below). Agency staff expanded to offices in nearby town houses.

In 1941, REA occupied new headquarters (above) at 1201 Connecticut Avenue. A year later, the war took the agency to St. Louis and the Boatmens National Bank Building (right), where sign (top left) warmly welcomed staff. Left: REA housewarming party at 1201 Connecticut, January, 1941.

'The War': Change of Address and Role for REA

As the war-threatening year 1941 drew to a close, nearly one million farms were receiving power from more than 800 co-ops financed by REA; nearly 35 percent of all farms were electrified. Now, there was intense momentum to push on, to complete the job. But most people in rural electrification sensed an interruption in the offing. War clouds were curtailing most of America's plans and aspirations, including REA's.

In 1941 the REA circus introduced a defense theme, the "Electro-Economy." Increase farm production electrically. Meet America's defense goals. Provide food for friends and allies defending freedom overseas.

The defense effort finally folded the REA circus tents forever on December 2, 1941. The action was prophetic. Five days later, the nation—and REA—was at war. Pearl Harbor. REA shifted from a preparedness role to the war posture—and to its World War II home. Destination: St. Louis.

1

Right: A St. Louis Star-Times *news photographer met the train of the last REA arrivals from Washington at the St. Louis Union Station on March 27, 1942. Host committees welcomed the federal employees and assisted them in locating housing. Above: Members of the REA state law unit in front of Boatmens National Bank Building, St. Louis home of REA, in June, 1942; from left: David Cohen, Lydia Bartz, Lora Cloninger, Yvonne Layton and Irlene Lewis.*

WOMEN'S PAGES SOCIETY NEWS

ST. LOUIS STAR-TIMES
MAGAZINE SECTION

RADIO PROGRAMS COMICS

ST. LOUIS, FRIDAY, MARCH 27, 1942.

Washington Loss—St. Louis Gain

Employes of the Rural Electrification Administration, a federal agency which is moving lock, **stock and barrel to St. Louis, picking out their grips upon arrival at the Union Station yesterday.**

2

St. Louis: Wartime Command Post of REA

In St. Louis, the REA staff, greatly reduced because of its men and women in the armed services, quickly adjusted to its wartime role. The agency assisted its borrowers in providing electric service to defense plants, Army and Navy installations and airstrips. It surveyed its borrowers and, along with the co-ops' new national organization, successfully convinced the War Production Board (WPB) that electrified farms dramatically pushed up food production. This brought WPB "go-aheads," enabling more farms to be connected during the war than otherwise would have been possible. REA's work in the food production effort played a big part in farmers meeting their production goals—minus the help of sons and daughters off to war, but greatly aided by their new on-farm electric hired hands and power from their REA co-ops. They successfully met and surpassed the ambitious and staggering wartime production goals placed upon them: 14 billion pounds of pork, 11 million head of cattle and calves, 122 billion pounds of milk in 1943.

Aware that the war-delayed construction of lines would create a tremendous "bottleneck" because of pent-up desires for electric service once the conflict was over, REA Administrator Slattery and staff started in 1943 to prepare a civilian "battle plan" of boldness and precision to meet postwar needs.

3

Despite the press of the war effort and reduced staff at REA, there was time for some frivolity during the St. Louis years. At left, Charles O. Falkenwald, who headed the successful national scrap drive by the co-ops for the war effort, got a bucket of it on his 41st birthday in January, 1943. Right: Arthur Gerth, popular and able director of REA's applications and loans division, was presented headdress recognizing his leadership prowess at 1943 Christmas party. Below left: Administrator Harry Slattery with Falkenwald at birthday party.

4

5

Right: Edgar D. Beach, manager, Maquoketa Valley Electric Cooperative, Manchester, Iowa, charted improved production with electric power at REA's "Food for Victory" conference in St. Louis, January, 1943. Below: Managers at conference with REA Administrator Slattery (seated at far left in black suit). Bottom right: REA General Counsel Vincent D. Nicholson at REA conference on postwar plans, 1943.

6

7

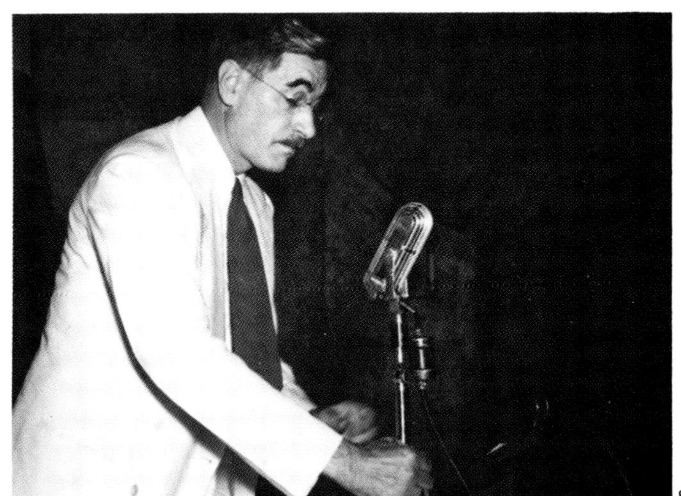

8

Left: Deputy REA Administrator William J. Neal presented the REA Production Award to the Ralph Childs family, November 13, 1943, as Mrs. Childs and sons Roger (far left) and Harold beamed proudly. Opposite page: Electricity helped Mrs. Childs whisk through housecleaning and hen house chores (top left and right) while electrically powered elevator cut down corn-unloading time for Ralph and Harold (lower left)—yielding more time for showing off the prize bull to visitors (lower right).

Middle left: Marquee of Manchester's Castle Theater, site of award ceremony, proclaiming the important event. City officials declared a local holiday that day as the Childs family captured national headlines, recognized as leading agricultural producers—aided by rural electric power—for the war effort. Above: Farm home of the Childs family which received light and power from lines of Maquoketa Valley Electric Cooperative at Manchester. Left: Electric power for the Childs' farm operations helped them raise more corn and grind more feed to meet expanded hog production—despite the loss of a hired hand and two sons off at war.

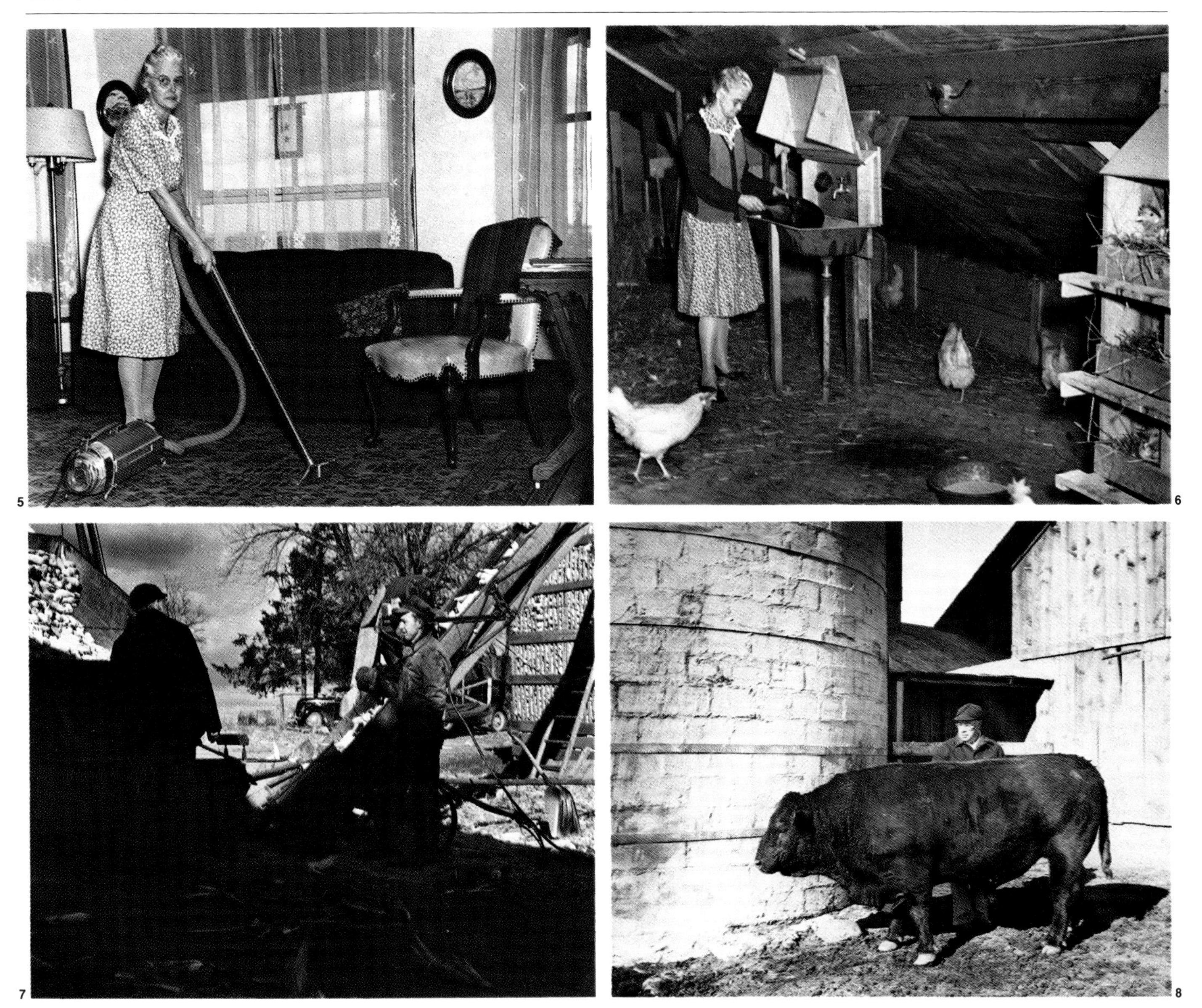
5 6 7 8

A Farm Family Powers Up for War

During World War II, farmers, allied with their electric "hired hands," broke one production record after another. Underscoring the need to use power under labor-scarce conditions and still meet war goals, REA instituted its "REA Production Award" to promote electric use.

In November, 1943, the Ralph Childs family, farming in Delaware County, Iowa, and a member of Maquoketa Valley Rural Electric Cooperative, was selected for the first presentation.

Using electric power wherever possible—electric milking machines, pumped water, brooders, heat lamps, feed grinding—the Childs in 1943 had doubled their dairy, beef, hog and poultry operations. At the same time, they were able to farm an additional 80 acres of corn to support the increased production—all this with the loss of their regular hired man off to war and two sons in the Army Air Corps.

The smiling faces of Mr. and Mrs. Daniel Flinn (couple in center) of Ashland, Illinois, and neighbors after getting a rare wartime electric "hookup." The Flinns, members of Menard Electric Co-op, Petersburg, got clearance after REA worked out a formula identifying productive farmers in late 1942. The drama of pre-war rural electrification was about to resume: the sign-ups and mappings, the meetings and building of the lines. Below: Rural women who would get co-op power before World War II huddled in September, 1939, to look for their place on REA line maps at Central Iowa 4-H Club Fair, Marshalltown, Iowa.

REA's fourth administrator, Agriculture Secretary Claude Wickard (right), was given oath of office by REA Personnel Director John Asher, St. Louis, July 12, 1945.

REA Begins Anew Amid Grief, Joy

The early months of 1945 took the nation on an emotional roller coaster. Optimism. Grief. Joy. Continued Allied advances after the successful Normandy invasion on D-Day brought soaring hopes that American boys would soon be coming home.

Even as spirits lifted, the nation was struck with grief and loss. On a warm spring day in April, President Roosevelt, working at his beloved Warm Springs cottage, died suddenly, signaling the end of an era. Soon the global conflict would be over.

In rural America, the big job would be resuming the effort to electrify the nation's farming regions—more than 50 percent still without power. REA, planning for this monumental task since early 1943, now had a new and energetic administrator, the vigorous wartime Secretary of Agriculture Claude Wickard, and was ready to begin anew.

The President with the people, Mandan, North Dakota, August, 1936. Below: Navy CPO Graham Jackson at FDR funeral procession, Warm Springs, Georgia, April, 1945.

FRANKLIN DELANO ROOSEVELT
January 30, 1882 April 12, 1945

Oh, Roosevelt, he was so great. That he would come out to our country when he did, to look at those conditions then, just an unheard of thing to do. But there he was amongst us. That time when he came out to South Dakota on the special train, he pulled a bunch of us into the railroad car, talked to us man to man. Now then, he pointed out the window over at the river (Missouri River). "There's your resource for power," he said, "the river has got to be developed, harnessed for power." Roosevelt changed our lives. He gave us *hope* (voice excited) and then he gave us the REA! Some hated him. But many of us worshipped him. . . .

—Emil Loriks, South Dakota farmer and New Deal activist, January, 1983

ATLAS
PERMA-GUARD
ANTI-FREEZE
Does not Evaporat
ROYAL CROWN
ROYAL CROWN
OLA

Coming of Age: The Boom Years

When Johnny comes marching home again . . . Head high, light of victory in his eye . . . Back to folks and sweetheart . . . Back to the farm . . . He won't be the same Johnny who went away . . . He's seen the face of modern war, known its awful might . . . In the jungles and on the beaches, Johnny fought to end the global nightmare . . . Saw to it that swords were turned to plowshares . . . Now Johnny turns his sights to building his tomorrow . . . And for him, the old way, the old drudgery of farm life and work, won't do in his tomorrow . . . For Johnny, the sword is a bazooka's steel melted down into a humming electric motor . . . Copper shell casings converted to singing rural electric lines . . . War dollars and a nation's energies turned to investments in a rural America powered and thriving with electric kilowatts . . . Investments in the tomorrows of the Johnnys of rural America . . . A rural America of light, of power, of opportunity.

Soldier visits with the home folks at Brown Summit, North Carolina, May, 1944.

Far right: G.L. Bridwell (with yardstick) and J.K. Smith, managers of adjacent systems in Kentucky, sorting out consumers who signed up with the wrong co-op for postwar rural electric power, 1945. Right: Illinois farmer discusses imminent ''hookup'' with lineman, 1945.

1

2

3

Above: Construction superintendent O.S. (''Smiley'') Hall (left) of Claiborne Electric Co-op, Homer, Louisiana, taking job applications from Sgt. Bill Brauch (center) and Signalman L.W. Walker, October, 1945. Veterans got preference for co-op jobs. Right: Awesome distances on snowy North Dakota prairie captured in this 1948 photo depicts big job ahead for REA. Below right: I.M. Johnson showing D.B. Lancaster, manager of Bowie-Cass Electric Co-op, Douglassville, Texas, locations of some 800 members he signed up, November, 1945. Left: Farmer signing up for power with Sekan Electric Co-op, Girard, Kansas, April, 1945.

4

5

6

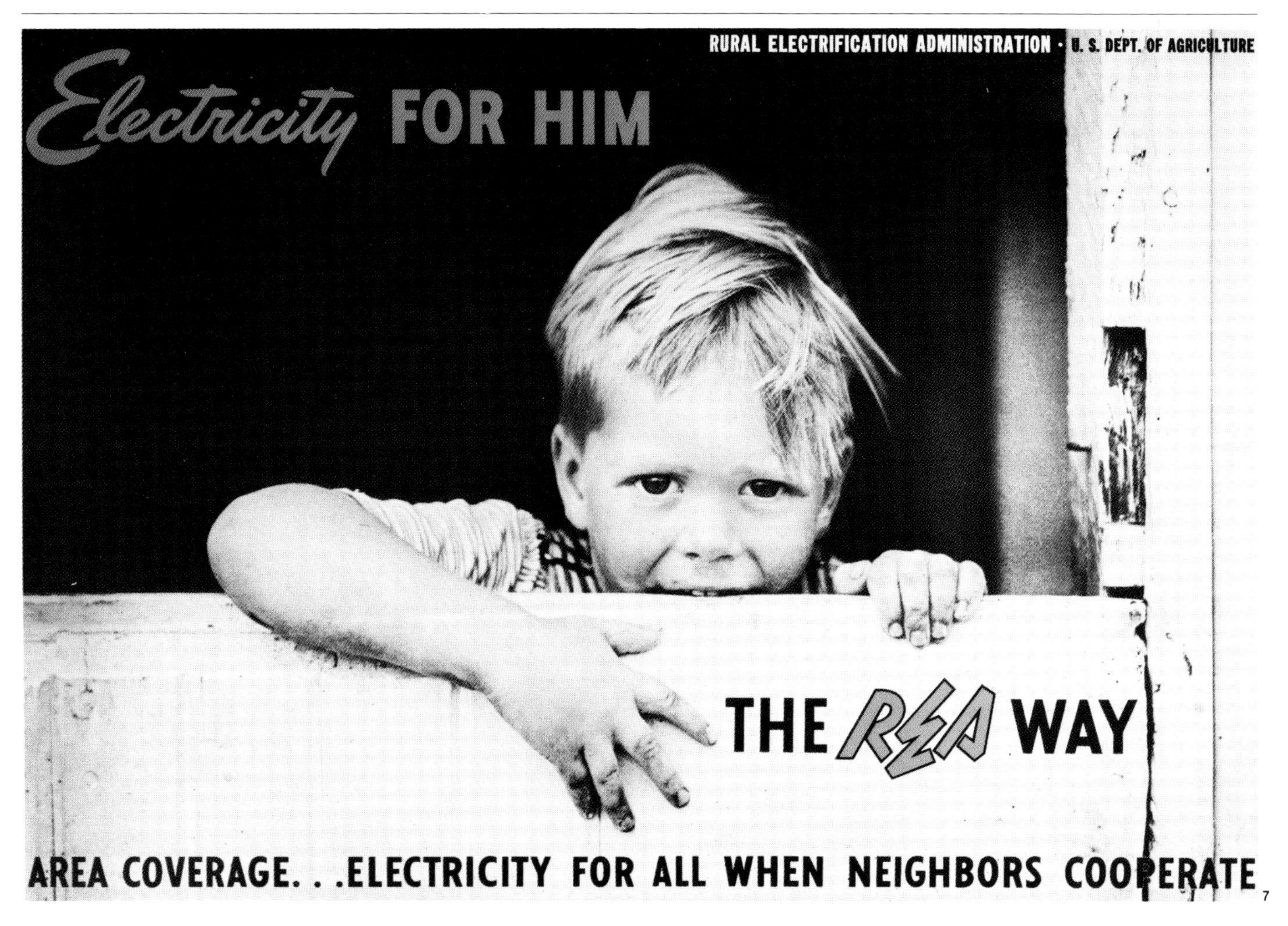

7

Green Light for Rural Electrification

After the war, nobody in America had to sell anybody on rural electrification or REA. Johnny was returning home from surroundings where electricity was taken for granted. And he had a lot to do with the enormous pent-up pressures that were being placed upon REA for electric service.

Veterans had become used to electric light and power in the induction and training camps, on battleships and in battle encampments around the globe. Johnny had changed, but so had REA. While war was being waged, REA had planned intensively for the anticipated postwar "boom," and it was ready to meet it.

Congress had also done its part for postwar rural electrification. In 1944, it passed the Department of Agriculture Organic Act, known as the Pace Act, making REA a permanent agency. But most importantly, it made possible "area coverage"—the covenant between Congress and the co-ops that electricity would be made available to all. The Pace Act abolished the old variable interest rate charged REA borrowers on past and future loans and set the new rate at two percent, and it stretched the pay-back period on REA loans from 25 to 35 years.

Now REA could bring power to those sparsely settled rural areas which previously could not meet economic tests. Rural electrification had the green light.

1

2

Crews from five Virginia co-ops moved into service area of Craig-Botetourt Electric Co-op April 30, 1948, to construct lines and counter takeover attempt by Appalachian Power Company, Roanoke. Above: Linemen of Shenandoah Valley Electric Co-op, Dayton, connected more than 200 consumers that day. Right: B-A-R-C Co-op linemen from Millboro making connection in Gala area. Below right: Linemen of Northern Virginia Electric Co-op installing transformer on farm near Manassas, December, 1946.

3

4

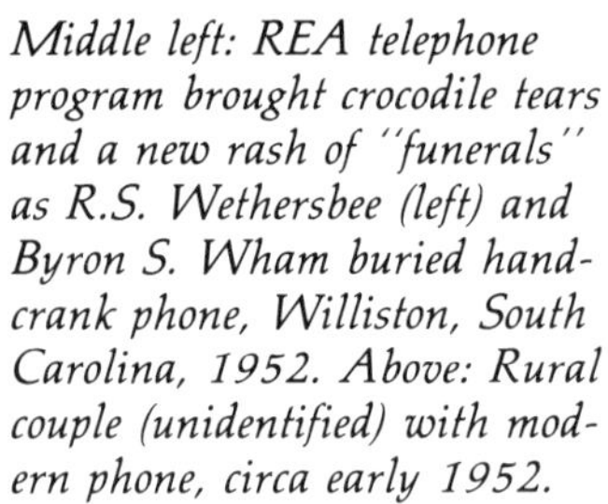

Middle left: REA telephone program brought crocodile tears and a new rash of "funerals" as R.S. Wethersbee (left) and Byron S. Wham buried handcrank phone, Williston, South Carolina, 1952. Above: Rural couple (unidentified) with modern phone, circa early 1952.

5

Left: Mr. and Mrs. Chester Williams, members of Gibson County Electric Membership Corporation, Trenton, Tennessee, register surprise and delight on July 28, 1949, at being presented a brand new washing machine. The occasion was a ceremony honoring the Fruitvale area farm couple as the one-millionth customer of the Tennessee Valley Authority (TVA). The ceremony brought out a distinguished assembly of federal and regional power officials to the Williams farm. On platform from left were Robert T. Hosman, president, TVA Electric Institute (standing at microphone); "States Rights" Finley, manager, Chattanooga Municipal Electric System; Dr. Knox Hutchinson, president, Tennessee Rural Electric Cooperative Association; William J. Neal, REA Deputy Administrator, and George O. Wessenauer, manager of public power, TVA.

Electricity for All—And Telephones, Too!

In 1947, REA Administrator Claude Wickard, striving to give Congress an idea of the enormous pressures for rural electric power out on the land, wrote Congressman Jamie Whitten of Mississippi:

"The first of this year, there were 2.5 million farm families still living without electric light and power. . . . Few counties, even in the less-densely settled areas of the West, have completed rural electrification . . . (and) it is a fact that almost 60 percent of the unelectrified farms are east of the Mississippi."

Congress heeded Wickard's request for funds. Hefty appropriations matched "boom years" demand. And after supply bottlenecks for poles, transformers and conductors were broken, line construction moved with dramatic swiftness across rural America.

By the end of 1948, more than 40,000 consumers a month were being connected to co-op lines, not only in the vast and isolated reaches of the Dakotas and Montana, but in the denser areas of the East where some had missed electricity the first time around.

In 1949, REA-financed co-ops energized 184,000 miles of electric line—more than 15,000 miles a month, nearly 700 miles a working day.

That was also the year Congress, with leadership from the Truman Administration, responded to the clamor of rural people for REA-financed rural telephone service. Fewer than 40 percent of all farms had phone service and most of those were antiquated "whoop and holler" affairs.

By 1950, more than one million miles of electric lines, financed by REA, had been energized and more than 75 percent of America's farms were electrified.

Cooperatives were making area coverage—electricity for all—a reality.

Left: Death-defying transmission construction crew installing conductor atop high voltage steel tower of Bonneville Power Administration along Columbia River, 1940. Right: Norris Dam of the Tennesse Valley Authority (TVA), named for Senator George W. Norris, legislative architect of spectacularly successful regional agency. Located on Tennessee's Clinch River, construction of Norris Dam was begun in 1933, was completed in 1936.

Left: TVA's Fontana Dam on the Little Tennessee River in North Carolina during night construction, 1944. Dam was built in just 13 months to meet power needs. Above: Drillers working on TVA's Fort Loudoun Dam, Loudon County, Tennessee, 1940.

Left: Public Works Administration (PWA) workers constructing a diversion tunnel to carry Missouri River water around earthworks of Fort Peck Dam, eastern Montana, 1936. Right: Workers of the PWA scaling rock cliffs in 1933 at site of Bonneville Dam on the Columbia River in the Pacific Northwest. Both construction projects were managed by the U.S. Army Corps of Engineers.

7

8

Left: East end of Grand Coulee Dam's west powerhouse, north central Washington, July, 1942. Nearly 250 million kilowatt hours went to Washington and Oregon co-ops and municipal and public agencies in 1942 from the Bonneville and Grand Coulee power systems, marketed by the Bonneville Power Administration. Production doubled and tripled in succeeding war years.
Above: The 200-ton, 74-foot shaft of no. nine generator, Grand Coulee's west powerhouse, April, 1948.

Federal Power and 'Preference': Helping Hands to Co-ops

After 1945, huge federal hydroelectric projects, begun during the New Deal and war years, continued to come on line. Developments nearing completion included the U.S. Bureau of Reclamation's giant Grand Coulee Dam in the Pacific Northwest and additional installations of the Tennessee Valley Authority (TVA).

Still, the nation's electric generators—both private and public—strained to meet the booming postwar growth. Rural electric co-ops were almost totally dependent on outside power suppliers and as the growth mushroomed, wholesale power shortages became rural electrification's overriding concern.

New hydro projects were inaugurated. President Harry S Truman and a cooperative Congress, well aware that rural electrification could not be finally achieved without federal power's helping hand, authorized power developments in the Southwest and Southeast.

And up and down the Missouri River Basin, the U.S. Army Corps of Engineers was building a 1944-authorized series of multipurpose dams for power and irrigation in the High Plains states.

Federal lawmakers since 1906 had provided, as an anti-monopoly measure, that public bodies be given the first call—"preference"—in the sale of power from federal dams. Cooperatives were added as entities eligible for preference in the TVA Act in 1933, and they have been included in all subsequent federal water and power statutes.

This meant that the cooperatives—latecomers to the power industry and thus "captive" customers to private suppliers—had recourse to wholesale power at reasonable rates. It also meant that the federal power supplied to the co-ops created a competitive and counter-monopoly "yardstick" for measuring power rates.

Power Supply: David and Goliath Battle

Rural electric systems had joined together in federations, called generation and transmission cooperatives or "G&Ts," as early as 1936 to obtain REA financing and meet wholesale power needs. The crucial issue of power supply caused them to bring into play one of the great principles of cooperative enterprise—"cooperation among cooperatives."

In the postwar boom years, as rural electrification emerged as a strong national movement, power company opposition to G&T loans became intense. Only the issue of preference in the sale of federal power for the cooperatives produced more heat. Up until the 1960s, REA would make a loan to a generation and transmission co-op only after lawsuits and extensive wrangling with the Congress. Often, the loan was made only after a compromise or "partnership" arrangement between the warring parties was struck.

Looking at the figures, it's difficult to understand why the companies viewed the co-ops as a threat. In 1945, when the companies boasted more than 40,000 megawatts of generation, the co-ops had 96. In 1950, the companies' combined capacity was 55,000 megawatts, the cooperatives' 412; in 1955, the score was 86,887 to 851. But the philosophical battle raged for another decade and more before subsiding.

By the late 1950s, it became clear that the co-ops needed large additions of generation and transmission (G&T) capacity—their own wholesale power—if future demands of rural electric consumers were going to be met. Use of electric power by co-op members was outstripping the hydro power capacity of the dams. Over the decade, rural electric annual growth had nearly quadrupled as kilowatt-hour sales zoomed from 6.8 billion in 1950 to more than 26 billion by 1960.

The G&T cooperatives, facing an imminent power shortage, were in a bind. They were told by federal power officials in the Eisenhower Administration that they were on their own when it came to power supply. Yet these were the same officials responsible for the "no new starts" policies on federal water and power projects. Something had to give.

Above right: E.D.H. Farrow, President of Brazos Electric Power Cooperative, Waco, Texas, opening steam valve to start turbine and dedicate new 11,500 kilowatt steam generating plant in ceremonies at Belton in March, 1950. The plant (above), named in honor of Texas Congressman W.R. Poage, initially met a large part of the power needs of Brazos Electric's 19 member distribution co-ops and 48,000 rural Texas families.

Right: Alex B. Veech, President of East Kentucky Power Cooperative, speaking at dedication of 44,000 kilowatt William C. Dale Station at Ford, December, 1954. Seated behind Veech is REA Administrator Ancher Nelsen. REA G&T loans in the 1950s were made after "differences" between local investor-owned utilities and cooperatives were resolved and "partnership arrangements" struck.

Right: North Dakota Senator Milton R. Young speaking at groundbreaking for 30,000 kilowatt generating station of Central Power Electric Cooperative at Voltaire, North Dakota, May, 1950. The co-op plant, fueled by North Dakota lignite, raised the state's generating capacity by one-third when entering operation in 1952. Middle right: First REA G&T loans were made in 1936 for Reeve diesel generating station of Federated Power Cooperative Association, Hampton, Iowa, and the plant (below) of Central Electric Federated Cooperative Association, Pocahontas, Iowa.

4

5

6

7

Above: Engine room of Chippewa Falls diesel generating station of Wisconsin Power Cooperative, 1940. Throughout the 1930s and '40s, small diesel plants comprised the generating capacity of the rural electric generation and transmission systems. By 1945, they boasted a combined capacity of 96 megawatts. Right: Modern exterior of 6,000 kilowatt steam plant at Genoa, Wisconsin, operated by Tri-State Power Cooperative, La-Crosse, 1941. Tri-State had evolved out of Wisconsin Power Cooperative, later to become Dairyland Power Cooperative.

8

Above left: The 22,000 kilowatt generating plant of Eastern Iowa Light & Power, Wilton, when it came on line in 1959. Above right: Open house in November, 1960, for nuclear power reactor owned and operated by Rural Cooperative Power Association, Elk River, Minnesota. Left: Dispatcher in control room where 1,300 separate points are monitored at 1,200,000 kilowatt, coal-fired New Madrid plant of Associated Electric Cooperative, Springfield, Missouri.

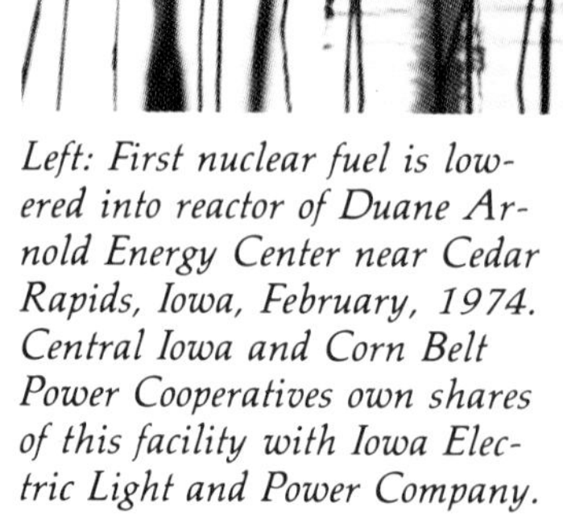

Left: First nuclear fuel is lowered into reactor of Duane Arnold Energy Center near Cedar Rapids, Iowa, February, 1974. Central Iowa and Corn Belt Power Cooperatives own shares of this facility with Iowa Electric Light and Power Company.

Above: Twin stacks of 230,000 kilowatt plant at Petersburg, Indiana, of Hoosier Energy Rural Electric Cooperative, Bloomington. Opposite page, bottom left: Switchyard carrying power from Petersburg plant to rural systems in southern Indiana.

The 'Big Stuff'

When Norman M. Clapp became REA Administrator in 1961, he acted boldly to place REA squarely in the power supply arena. His actions propelled rural electrification into a new era: the age of the "Super G&T" and the "Big Stuff" in generation and transmission.

The era of the "teakettle" generators was over, as were the old policies. Clapp declared there would be no more crippling "partnership" or "shotgun" arrangements surrounding G&T loans. Then he issued the landmark "third criterion" for power supply loans, making the "security and effectiveness" of the REA-financed systems a controlling guideline. It was a clear signal that REA was leaving behind its ambiguous and timid policies on G&T loans, giving the go-ahead for the co-ops to get on with their business of meeting their growing wholesale power and utility responsibilities. Hefty budgets for G&T loans, with approving nods from the Kennedy and Johnson White Houses, accelerated the program.

Above: Making a $30.5 million loan to Colorado-Ute Electric Association, at Montrose, Colorado, early in his administration, REA Administrator Norman M. Clapp termed the decision to build the 190,000 kilowatt Hayden Station the "beginning of a stronger, more secure and permanent pattern of rural electrification" at groundbreaking ceremonies for the plant on April 20, 1963.

Right: Ten-story mobile earth mover mining North Dakota lignite for power plant of Basin Electric Power Cooperative, Bismarck, North Dakota, symbolized coming of "Giant Power" for rural electrification in the early 1960s. Below: The three-unit, coal-fired, 1,650,000 kilowatt Laramie River Station of the Missouri Basin Power Project (MBPP) at Wheatland, Wyoming, is operated by Basin Electric, a regional G&T serving co-ops in eight states. The MBPP is a joint regional power venture involving co-ops and public power organizations.

The huge boiler furnaces begin to cool, the turbine blades begin their long spin down to inertness; silence strangely replaces the steady din throughout the power plant. It is time for annual maintenance overhaul at a G&T generating station. . . . Left: Operators of United Power Association's plant at Stanton, North Dakota, working on turbine section of turbine-generator. Below: Technician laboring over gear of electric motor using disassembled pulverizer as workbench. Opposite page, top left: Workers inspecting base of pulverizers which grind lignite to powder-fine dust for combustion in boiler. Top right: Inside the boiler, a welder mending tubing which make up its walls. Bottom: Workmen tightening huge bolt on turbine section of the turbine generator as the overhaul nears completion. This is the "Big Stuff."

1

2

With Power, a Confident Future

Electric power industry onslaughts against REA's stepped-up power supply program were strong until the end of the 1960s. But as REA Administrator David A. Hamil took the helm and indicated his unwavering support for a strong G&T program, resistance waned.

The "program" had moved through its struggling early years, a perilous period when survival alone marked success, then had weathered—magnificently—the halcyon "boom" years of great growth—and now in the 1970s and '80s, with assured supplies of power, suddenly found itself strong, confident, assured. Rural electrification had come of age.

3

4

5

Left: Crews of Surprise Valley Electrification Corp., California, erecting new lines in 1968. Right: John McGuffin, eastern New Mexico rancher and the five millionth rural electric consumer in 1962, talks on phone with Agriculture Secretary Orville Freeman.

Below: Linemen of Petit Jean Electric Cooperative, Arkansas, cut through mountain timber, used helicopter to build 26 miles of line in 1969 to tiny Ozark hamlets of Ben Hur, Raspberry Knob, Falling Water and Richland Creek.

Above: Mr. and Mrs. John McGuffin (left), owners of a small New Mexico cattle ranch near Tatum, became the five millionth rural electric consumer in 1962. The couple posed for photographers with R.B. Moore, manager of Lea County Electric Cooperative, Lovington, amid new appliances on July 2 at their ranch. Left: Clayton McNeill, 83, read Bible by light of kerosene lamp until June, 1984, when Blue Ridge Electric Membership Corp., North Carolina, brought electricity to his home outside community of Obids. Widower McNeill's austere lifestyle did not incline him to get electricity until he began having eye-trouble reading his Bible. After he got it, he gave a sort of testament, reflecting, "Electricity is like religion. My great-great uncle, Shadrack Calloway, told his brother, Ben, at his baptism that religion is a good thing. And Ben said, 'Yes, it's a damn good thing and I wish everybody had it.' I guess electricity is like that."

6

7

Above: REA Administrator David A. Hamil in 1969 at meter with Eskimo children at Grayling, Alaska, which got power that year. Right: REA Administrator Robert W. Feragen signs loan for Navajo Tribal Utility Authority (NTUA), Window Rock, Arizona, January, 1981. Loan made electric service possible for 2,100 families. At left is NTUA Manager Malcolm Dalton; at right, Chairman Leland R. Gardner. Below: Lloyd M. Hodson, Manager, Alaska Village Electric Co-op, Anchorage, points out remote spot in his vast service area.

8

Above: Taos Pueblo Indians beat message on ceremonial drums signaling that power has come from Kit Carson Electric Cooperative, Taos, on October 6, 1971. Below: Vinalhaven Island off coast of Maine got reliable electric service in 1977 through REA loan and islander-organized Fox Islands Electric Cooperative.

9

10

Building to the Last Frontier

Through mountain passes and up the narrow box canyons, in Ozark mountain villages and islands off the coast of Maine, across forbidding Nevada desert and icy Alaskan tundra, in ancient New Mexico pueblos—in all the forsaken places where rural people were still without power—the rural electric co-ops, now called the "RECs," continued their relentless advance.

You would see the tiny speck of a yellow truck far, far in the distance; then, the A-frame raising a pole. Light and power, coming for the first time. In the 1960s, '70s, even into the 1980s, that high and moving moment in rural people's lives was still being enacted. Rural electrification, begun as a people's cooperative movement to fill a need, still had that old magic and power, that special feeling, on days like this. Here on these last frontiers, and all across rural America, the job was not yet done, never will be.

WE PROTEST

Through Unity, Strength

The wires which tied the houses of rural people together also seemed to unite their spirits. Beginning in the early days and growing through the years, there has been some unusual quality about the rural electrification program which has drawn people of diverse political and social views together in a common purpose. The people who work for our program feel they're working in a cause or movement or a crusade which many of them can't define.

—From *A Giant Step*
by Clyde T. Ellis

When Clyde Ellis attempted to describe and define rural electrification's power and appeal as a national program and movement in 1966, he had been that movement's leader and chief advocate for nearly 25 years. Since 1942, when the National Rural Electric Cooperative Association (NRECA) had been formed with Ellis as its head, the man and the organization had led rural electrification through turbulent times of great and often bitter conflict. Epic national battles were waged—and won—in the defense and advance of that "cause," which, nearly a quarter century later, still fascinated and compelled Ellis and the millions committed to it.

All through the Ellis years, and under later successors, NRECA recommendations to Congress for REA loan funds most often won out over cut-and-slash proposals submitted by often-hostile White House budgeters.

The record of NRECA in those years, stamped with the strong and powerful personality of Ellis and his spellbinding, single-minded leadership, is studded with stunning victories, few defeats.

These were the fabled years of political conflict—the budget battles and fights over White House control of REA funds; fierce and free-wheeling propaganda wars with the power companies; giant battles over federal power—"preference" rights for NRECA's co-op members, fights for "all-Federal" transmission and for REA G&T loans; battle cries and calls to arms over "Dixon-Yates," "Clark Hill" and "Hell's Canyon"—water resource give-aways to private interests—all conflicts that would have a way of repeating themselves in later decades.

The NRECA "clout" nationally and on Capitol Hill went right back home to the grass-roots. It was the power of those folks on the lines, their co-ops and "statewide" organizations—still working for that "cause" Ellis couldn't quite define—that made them a force to be reckoned with. It was clout they would need in the years just ahead.

Opposite: Some 1,400 rural electric leaders gathered in Washington's Mayflower Hotel on January 23, 1973, to protest the Nixon Administration's termination of the Rural Electrification Administration's loan program.

Steve Tate, Georgia

E.J. Stoneman, Wisconsin

E.D.H. Farrow, Texas

Harry Edmunds, Minnesota

Robert D. Tisinger, Georgia

Thomas Fitzhugh, Arkansas

Above and at top, opposite: Nine of the ten incorporators of NRECA. Tisinger was not an incorporator, but was present; he was associate general counsel, then replaced Fitzhugh as general counsel.

The incorporators met in the Willard Hotel (right), the Washington landmark now being rebuilt, to draw up bylaws. No picture of incorporator William Jackman, New Jersey, could be located.

'To Make Their Voices Heard'

REA geared itself to provide considerable management and technical assistance to the new cooperatives, but some problems they had to tackle by themselves.

"To make their voices heard," Clyde T. Ellis, NRECA's first general manager, recalled years later, "rural electric leaders soon realized they must speak in unison."

The first response was to organize statewide associations. By 1937, these were active in a handful of states and in 1943 there were 21. They secured passage of state laws affecting the program and provided many joint services.

But some problems cried out for a unified national voice. Among these in the early months of World War II were material shortages and the inability to get needed insurance at reasonable rates.

At the urging of interested members of Congress, and with the tacit encouragement of some REA officials, rural electric leaders from across the nation met in Washington early in 1942 to discuss forming a national organization. Ten of them incorporated the National Rural Electric Cooperative Association on March 19. The next day they met at Washington's historic Willard Hotel to adopt bylaws, elect officers and accept memberships.

On September 18, the board met in St. Louis and announced that the association had 144 member systems. In November it had grown to 266 members.

NRECA quickly formed its own insurance companies, but this move sparked controversy and eventual opposition from REA. As co-op leaders had learned when they began building their own electric lines, competition brought results. They soon were able to negotiate coverages from a commercial company.

Getting materials was tougher, but the co-ops did convince government officials that electricity could replace lost manpower and help increase food production. Earlier severe restrictions were then eased.

8 *Raymond Walker, Missouri*

9 *J.C. Nichols, Wyoming*

10 *Dolph H. Wolf, Michigan*

11 *Will Hall Sullivan, Tennessee*

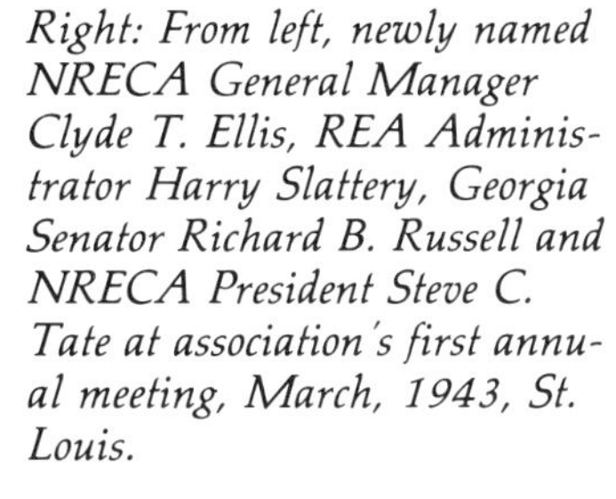

Right: From left, newly named NRECA General Manager Clyde T. Ellis, REA Administrator Harry Slattery, Georgia Senator Richard B. Russell and NRECA President Steve C. Tate at association's first annual meeting, March, 1943, St. Louis.

12

13

Left: Eugene Casey, special assistant to President Roosevelt, brought White House greetings to NRECA's first annual meeting. Right: Steve C. Tate, Georgia, was elected the first president of NRECA and presided at the meeting.

14

15

Above: REA Administrator Harry Slattery (left) with gold watch presented to Nebraska Senator George Norris, honored for his contributions to rural electrification.

Right: Mississippi Representative John Rankin, another who was instrumental in gaining passage of legislation creating REA, spoke at the first annual meeting.

16

Right: Clyde T. Ellis early in the 1960s. Below: Ellis (second from right) at first NRECA annual meeting in 1943, two weeks after becoming the association's first general manager. Others at meeting were Senator George Norris (at lectern), NRECA President Steve Tate (right).

1

2

Right: Ellis and Wyoming Senator Joseph C. O'Mahoney debating power issues with New York Representative William E. Miller and Edwin Vennard, a long-time power company foe of Ellis. Dwight Stone, center, was host of the CBS radio program in the mid-1950s.

3

4

5

Above: North Dakota Senator William Langer talking with CIO President Walter Reuther and Ellis during a workshop meeting of the influential Electric Consumers Information Committee in Washington in 1954.

6

Above: 1952 and 1956 Democratic Presidential candidate Adlai Stevenson (near flag) joined Ellis at a 1956 meeting of Electric Consumer Information Committee. Others include: Dewey Anderson (right) of Public Affairs Institute, and Clay Cochran (in corner), ECIC coordinator. Left: Ellis welcoming Texas Senator Lyndon B. Johnson to 1957 NRECA annual meeting in Chicago. Looking on were Texas Director R.A. Yarbrough, NRECA President John M. George (rear) and Secretary-Treasurer Albert C. Hauffe (right).

7

Left: A bare-footed Ellis during a tour of India to determine prospects for rural electrification. Right: This photo of Harry S Truman and Ellis possibly taken at an NRECA regional meeting in Kansas City after Truman had retired. Below left: Ellis (center), United Auto Worker Vice President Pat Greathouse (below), Farmers Union President James Patton (left) and Kenneth Holum leaving John F. Kennedy's Georgetown home shortly after 1960 Presidential election. The three discussed power policies with Kennedy; Holum was later named Assistant Secretary of the Interior for Water and Power.

8

Below: "Mister Rural Electrification" received a standing ovation at a Washington dinner honoring him in January, 1968. To Ellis' right is his wife, Camille; at lectern is Vice President Hubert Humphrey.

9

10

'Mr. Rural Electrification'

Perhaps no person left his mark more indelibly on rural electrification than Clyde T. Ellis.

Among those who had met with the incorporators of NRECA in March, 1942, was Ellis, then a fiery young Arkansas Congressman and advocate of rural electrification and water-resource development. The incorporators liked what they saw and heard. Later that year, after Ellis had lost a bid for a U.S. Senate seat, they asked him to become the first NRECA general manager. He accepted and began his duties at the close of his Congressional term in January, 1943.

It was Ellis who insisted that the national organization be controlled at the grass-roots, but it was also he who was out front and who convinced the members to take surprisingly strong stands on rural electrification and water and power policy that invariably resulted in a stronger rural electrification movement.

An inspiring orator, his speeches to members often lasted two hours—and no one wanted to miss them.

After 25 years as chief executive officer of the association, Ellis—slowed only slightly by the effects of a crippling stroke—stepped down. In that time the association had grown from a "one-man gang" to national prominence based on his leadership and the unified support of its members.

Right: Mid-West Electric Consumers Association, Denver, Colorado, responded to the termination of the REA program with a special edition. Below: USDA press release December 29, 1972, was first word of the Administration plan.

MID-WEST Electric Consumers Association NEWS

Bulk Rate
U.S. Postage
PAID
Bismarck, N.D.
Permit No. 224
Address Correction Requested

Volume 6, Number 1 | 10395 West Colfax Avenue, Denver, Colorado 80215 | January 1973

Rural America Up In Arms

NIXON KILLS 2% REA LOANS

1

Jennings (202) 447-5606
McDavid (202) 447-4026

NEWS

U. S. DEPARTMENT OF AGRICULTURE

RURAL ELECTRIC AND RURAL TELEPHONE LOAN PROGRAMS CHANGE:

WASHINGTON, Dec. 29—The U.S. Department of Agriculture announced today that the REA electric and telephone 2 percent direct loan programs are being converted to insured and guaranteed loan programs at somewhat higher interest rates effective Jan. 1, 1973. This action was made possible by the enactment of the Rural Development Act of 1972 in which the Congress provided very broad authorities to make guaranteed and insured loans to finance all types of community development programs.

This change is a part of the effort to hold 1973 Federal budget outlays to $250 billion and keep the outstanding public debt within the statutory limit of $465 billion through June 30, 1973. It will eliminate direct Federal loans and substitute credit from private sources at interest rates that are more in line with the cost of money on today's market. Insured and guaranteed loans will reduce the impact on the Federal budget and the public debt and are designed to facilitate more rapid growth in the credit programs being provided by the National Rural Utilities Cooperative Finance Corporation, the Rural Telephone Bank and other private lenders.

Beginning on Jan. 1, 1973, all REA loans will be made as guaranteed and insured loans under the authority of Section 104 of the Rural Development Act of 1972 (Section 306(a)(1) of the Consolidated Farm and Home Development Act). In order to meet more fully the needs of REA borrowers, an additional $200 million in loan authority will be made available over and above current allocations. This will provide a total loan authority of $618 million for rural electric loans and $145 million for rural telephone loans in fiscal year 1973. These funds are in addition to those loans available to REA borrowers from private sources, including CFC.

Loans to electric and telephone cooperatives will be made on an insured basis at 5 percent interest (guaranteed loans will also be available on advantageous terms). Loans to commercial power companies and commercial telephone companies will be guaranteed at market rates of interest.

Many details of this transition from the authorities of the Rural Electrification Act of 1936, as amended, to the authorities of the Rural Development Act will require time to work out. Borrowers and other interested parties will be advised of the necessary changes in loan requirements and loan processing as rapidly as possible. Every effort will be made to expedite these new programs in order to meet the expanding needs of REA borrowers.

\- - - - - - - -

6143 USDA 4212-72

2

3

4

Above and left: Minnesota Senator Hubert Humphrey rose from a sick bed to speak at the Mayflower Hotel rally. He was wildly cheered as he exhorted them: "You embattled farmers can do in the year 1973 for free government, for representative government, what others almost 200 years before have done. You can use this program, the REA program, as a test of the legitimacy of whether or not one man, by executive order, can ignore the expressed will of the American people through Congress assembled. You can determine for once and all whether or not a President can continue to impound funds that have been appropriated by Congress. You can strike a blow for freedom, for liberty and for constitutional government."

Below: President Nixon created an uproar in rural America on January 31, 1973. At a televised press conference he justified cutting off REA loans by declaring that 80 percent of the loans were going for "country clubs and dilettantes . . . and others who can afford living in the country."

6

5

Above: Pennsylvania rural electric leaders leaving the Rayburn House Office Building after visiting Pennsylvania representatives. Right: NRECA General Manager Robert D. Partridge and Minnesota Senator Hubert Humphrey during session at the Mayflower Hotel in January, 1973.

7

Rural Electrification's 'Black Friday'

REA was born in politics," said a former legislator, "and if it dies, it will die in politics."

A reminder came at 4 p.m., December 29, 1972, a day rural electric people call "Black Friday."

Just as the long New Year's weekend was beginning, the Nixon Administration terminated the REA loan program. A press release issued by the U.S. Department of Agriculture declared loans would no longer be made under the Rural Electrification Act. Instead, they would be made at higher interest rates under a new Rural Development Act.

Simultaneously, the Administration was refusing to spend authorized funds for other programs, many of them rural, precipitating what some called a "Constitutional crisis."

In the next 20 weeks, rural electric people demonstrated their battle-seasoned tempering developed from years of legislative conflict. President Dwight D. Eisenhower's 1959 veto of the Humphrey-Price bill to restore REA loan-making authority came to mind. The rural electric movement had sent a signal of its power then. The Senate, in near-unprecedented action, overrode the veto, the House coming within four votes. The close vote cooled a drive to pass crippling REA legislation.

This time, 1,400 of them flocked to Washington in late January, 1973, to protest the action. Armed with "We Protest" and "Save Rural Electrification" stickers and with kerosene lanterns and placards, they visited the offices of nearly every senator and representative to plead their case.

They returned again in May to urge Congress to pass new legislation restoring REA. It did, by an overwhelming margin.

The legislation created a new lending pro-

Left: NRECA General Manager Robert D. Partridge (right) conferred with Senator George Aiken of Vermont about legislation which eventually restored REA loans. Aiken, along with Senator Hubert Humphrey of Minnesota, introduced the legislation. Below: REA Administrator David A. Hamil had the unpleasant task of defending the Administration's suspension of his agency's loan program at NRECA's annual meeting in late February, 1973.

Above: Charles A. Robinson (left), NRECA staff counsel, with Montana Senator Lee Metcalf, chairman, and Win Turner, special subcommittee counsel, after testimony against impoundments at a Senate subcommittee hearing. Left: Senator Gale McGee of Wyoming announced his Agricultural Appropriations Subcommittee would not hear U.S. Department of Agriculture budget requests unless the Administration restored funding for programs such as REA.

gram. Instead of being reliant on the original direct-loan program dependent on annual Congressional authorizations and executive whim, the program now had a revolving fund into which flowed repayment of interest and principal and out of which new loans could be made.

Interest rates had been pegged at two percent since REA was made permanent in 1944. The new rates were higher, generally five percent for insured loans from the revolving fund and at the cost of federal borrowing (plus a service charge) for guaranteed loans, another type created.

President Richard Nixon signed the bill into law on May 11, 1973, the 38th anniversary of REA.

"A smashing victory," NRECA General Manager Robert D. Partridge called it, one that demonstrated that rural electric people had molded themselves into a force that wouldn't let REA "die in politics."

5

Above: W.R. (Bob) Poage of Texas (right), chairman of the House Agriculture Committee, during hearings on new REA legislation. Others (from left) are South Dakota Representative Frank E. Denholm, NRECA President Charles Wyckoff of Ohio, and NRECA General Manager Robert D. Partridge. Denholm introduced the legislation which eventually restored REA lending. Right: The controversy over termination of REA loans ended quietly on the 38th anniversary of the creation of the Rural Electrification Administration. On May 11, 1973, President Richard M. Nixon signed bill restoring the loan program. Watching (from left) are William Erwin, assistant secretary of agriculture for rural development, REA Administrator David A. Hamil, and Agriculture Secretary Earl L. Butz.

6

1

A traditional role of NRECA has been to survey its member rural electric co-ops and then inform the Congress what the capital needs for the coming fiscal year will be. Left: The Legislative Committee reviewing testimony on loan fund needs in 1969. Middle left: NRECA General Manager Clyde T. Ellis gesturing to Wyoming Senator Joseph C. O'Mahoney during a 1959 hearing.

2

3

4

Above: A 1963 Senate hearing on REA appropriations brought both power company officials and rural electric leaders to Washington. Identifiable rural electric leaders include: Oliver Rose, South Dakota (standing); John Ford, Alabama (fourth from right); R.B. Moore (second from right) and Carl Turner (right), both of New Mexico. Left: Helge Nygren of North Dakota and Art Jones of South Dakota testifying in 1967. Rural electrics are not united on all issues; in this case the Dakotans opposed legislation sought by other co-ops to create a rural electric bank.

Right: REA Administrator David A. Hamil (back to camera in front of man holding pencil by his head) making point before a Senate Agriculture subcommittee in 1971 as Senators Quentin Burdick of North Dakota (behind Hamil), James Allen of Alabama (to Burdick's left) and Subcommittee Chairman George McGovern of South Dakota, listened.

5

6

Left: Leroy Schecher, a South Dakota co-op manager, telling a House oversight committee about dire economic trouble in rural America, as evidenced by a scrapbook with 320 auction sale ads which appeared over a 47-day period in 1982. Right: NRECA General Manager Robert D. Partridge (right) testified with Colorado-Ute counsel Girts Krumins (left) and REA Administrator Robert W. Feragen at a 1980 hearing on co-op rate structures.

7

The Farmer-Director and the Congressman

In the late 1950s, a rural electric director from Iowa, calling on his congressman, was explaining the different problems associated with wholesale power as opposed to electric distribution. Asked one technical question after another, the director continued to supply answers until finally the congressman offhandedly asked where he had gotten his "E.E." (electrical engineering) degree. "Oh, no," the farmer replied. He had no college degree of *any* kind. "You just have to know these things if you're going to be a rural electric director."

Here was perhaps the best illustration of why the rural electrification program and NRECA's legislative agenda met with success on Capitol Hill. It was because of the grass-roots nature of the cooperatives and the rural electric program. Farmer-directors entered the legislative halls and chambers of Washington's mighty, stating their needs for the electric co-ops in such plausible ways and in such convincing terms that it was well-nigh impossible for the "program" to be denied.

And here was why other "interest groups," often much better equipped with financial resources, high-powered attorneys and other levers of influence, would turn green with envy at the legislative achievements of rural electrification.

1

Left: Texas Congressman W.R. Poage in his office meeting with co-op leaders. Right: South Dakotan Robert Martin visited House Speaker Tip O'Neill in 1973 as part of a co-op "adopt an urban congressman" program. Below: REA Administrator David A. Hamil describing rural electric issues to Colorado Senator Gary Hart.

2

3

4

Left: North Carolina delegation meeting with Senator Sam Ervin in 1974. Lower left: Indiana statewide association leaders waiting for an appointment with a member of their Congressional delegation. Below: Missouri Senator Thomas Eagleton discussing rural electrification with home-state co-op leaders.

5

6

Right: Chub Ulmer (second from right), North Dakota association manager, and Mississippi state manager Howard Langfitt (right), talking with Mississippi Congressman Jamie Whitten (left) and North Dakota Senator Mark Andrews, key figures in determining REA loan levels. Below: Georgia delegation meeting with Senator Herman Talmage (right, at table). Lower right: Minnesotans meeting with Vice President Walter Mondale.

7

8

9

Carrying a Grass-Roots Message to Congress

During the formative years of NRECA, its legislative thrust in Washington was aimed at crucial twin issues of increased REA loan funds and federal power development—needed for financing and building co-op lines and to assure future supplies of "preference" hydro power.

Those were the years of high-stakes legislation in Congress over live-or-die issues for rural electrification and NRECA. And, already, directors and managers of NRECA's member co-op systems were in the thick of legislative battle. Their active involvement soon gained NRECA the reputation as a "grass-roots" national organization—achieving legislative goals not so much through power and influence, but by mobilizing groundswells of popular support for a very popular program.

Directors and managers of NRECA member co-ops have become familiar figures on Capitol Hill. They testify before House and Senate committees, call on congressmen, and working through NRECA committees and legislative staff, map strategies for upcoming legislative agendas—all mandated by the one member, one vote bylaws of the NRECA resolutions process.

Throughout the 1970s and '80s, NRECA has made a dramatic annual show of back-home strength on Capitol Hill. During a full week of legislative conferences each May, upwards of 2,000 rural electric leaders arrive on "the Hill" and in statewide delegations call on their members, attend committee hearings and brief key legislative aides. They also make a special point of visiting and briefing urban congressmen about issues and needs of the program.

Noting one of these outpourings of rural electric people late one May afternoon in 1981, a senator holding hearings looked up from the table and remarked wryly, "Looks like every third person on this Hill today is wearing a rural electric button."

1

2

President Harry S Truman, "Uncle" John Hobbs (a co-op director, at left), and Governor Sid McMath, at dedication of Bull Shoals Dam in Arkansas, July 2, 1952. The project was bitterly opposed by commercial power companies. Truman lashed out at them and declared: "This power ought to go to lighten the burden of farmers and workers and housewives."

Above: Truman greets NRECA's Clyde Ellis at a meeting of the Electric Consumers Information Committee during 1958 visit to Washington. Right: He was a surprise guest speaker at NRECA's Region I meeting in Washington, September, 1948.

3

Right: NRECA Georgia Director Walter Harrison (left) and General Manager Clyde Ellis with President Dwight D. Eisenhower at the association's 1959 annual meeting in Washington. Two future presidents—John F. Kennedy and Lyndon B. Johnson—also addressed the meeting. Below: In 1965 Eisenhower attended the 25th anniversary meeting of Adams Electric Cooperative in Pennsylvania; the former President was a member of the co-op at his Gettysburg farm; Adams Electric officials, from left: Henry Miller, V. Kyle Trout, Benjamin Gayman, Eisenhower, William F. Matson, W.G. Hensel.

5

4

Rural Electrification and the White House

From Franklin D. Roosevelt to today, the President of the United States has always expressed an interest in rural electrification. Some of them, however, especially those with a rural background, have felt a special affinity.

Harry S Truman was a surprise visitor at several rural electric meetings. At one he presented NRECA officials with an old kerosene lantern and later scrawled a note to go along with it: "That old lantern is the one we used to carry around at four o'clock in the morning when the old man made us get up and feed the horses."

Dwight D. Eisenhower was a member of Adams Electric Cooperative, Pennsylvania, but when he spoke at the 1959 NRECA annual meeting, his proposal for higher REA interest rates was coolly received.

John F. Kennedy, although without a rural background, strongly backed an expanded program of loans for rural electric generating plants.

Lyndon B. Johnson had stronger ties to rural electrification than any other President. His single-minded determination as a Texas Congressman resulted in an electric co-op in his home county.

Jimmy Carter often recalled that his father was an incorporator and director of Sumter Electric Membership Corporation, Georgia, and credited the coming of electricity with allowing him to broaden his horizons.

Left: Officials of NRECA and American Public Power Association at White House meeting on natural resource development, September, 1963. From left: Assistant Secretary of Interior Ken Holum; Orville Freeman, Secretary of Agriculture; J. Dillon Kennedy and R.J. McMullin, APPA; Paul Tidwell, NRECA; Stewart Udall, Secretary of the Interior; Albert Hauffe, NRECA; Kennedy; Clyde T. Ellis, NRECA; Alex Radin, APPA.

After his unsuccessful attempt at the 1956 vice presidential nomination, John F. Kennedy was determined to improve his standing with rural people and westerners and took every opportunity to meet with them. Right: In 1958, he attended a meeting of the NRECA board to learn more about rural electrification. Above: At the 1960 Western States Water and Power Consumers Conference in Billings, Montana, with his sister, Eunice Shriver. His speech, often called "the Billings speech" by backers of federal power, was enthusiastically received and became a blueprint for development in his Administration. Above, right: Dedicating Oahe Dam at Pierre, South Dakota, August, 1962.

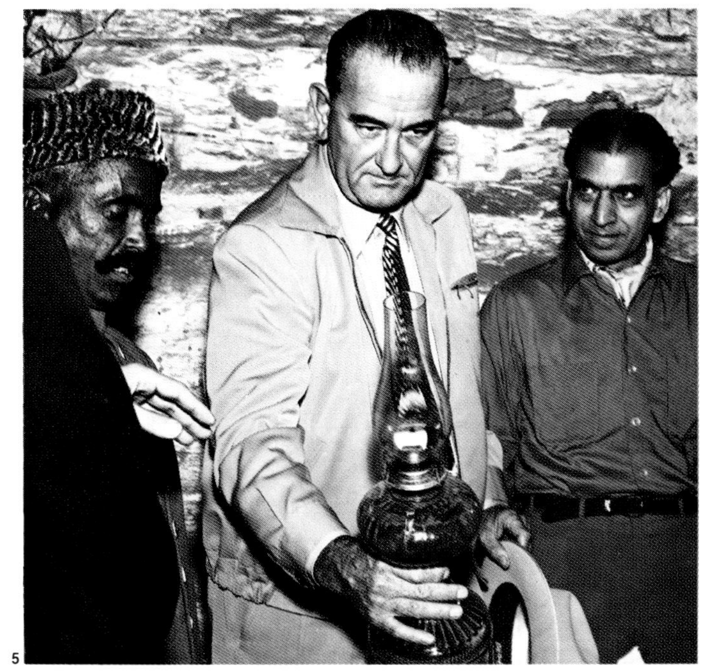

Of all the presidents, Lyndon B. Johnson was closest to rural electrification. He pushed hard to get REA to loan the money for Pedernales Electric Cooperative in his home county and finally cajoled President Roosevelt into ordering the loan, even though it didn't meet feasibility standards. Later, as President, he remained close to the cooperative and often visited it, and he was a frequent visitor at NRECA or Texas rural electric meetings. Left: The President examining a kerosene lamp in the log cabin in which he was born at the LBJ Ranch. Right: Addressing a meeting of Texas electric co-ops in 1952.

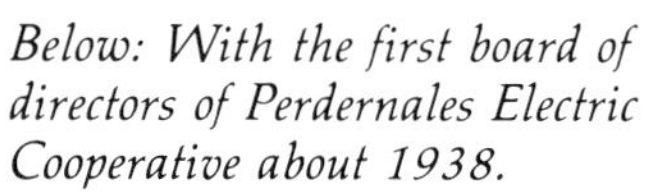

Below: With the first board of directors of Perdernales Electric Cooperative about 1938.

Above: Lady Bird and Lyndon Johnson were among those at the 5th birthday party of REA in 1940. At right is REA Administrator Harry Slattery. Right: NRECA staff members had a private visit with the President at the White House in 1964. From left: Jerry Anderson, Erma Angevine, Charles A. Robinson, Robert I. Kabat, William Murray, Robert Smith, Jake Lewis, Carl Laing, Robert D. Partridge, Clyde Ellis, William S. Roberts, Kermit Overby.

Left: Vice President Richard M. Nixon (seated, near lectern) at REA's 20th birthday, 1955. Administrator Ancher Nelsen (at lectern) telephoned Iowan Ben K. Hovland, a member of both a rural electric and a telephone co-op. Nixon said rural electrification was "the best example of the partnership principle between government and the people."

President Gerald R. Ford speaking to Rural Electric Youth Tour participants at the White House in 1976, one of two times he greeted the group. The tour is sponsored by local rural electric co-ops and is coordinated by NRECA. It attracts nearly 1,000 young people to Washington every year.

President Jimmy Carter greeted participants of 1978 Youth Tour on the White House lawn. "I grew up on a farm that didn't have any electricity," he had told the 1977 group. "I don't know how many of you ever milked cows by hand, or spent half the summer with a crosscut saw cutting oak wood for the fireplace, or chopping stove wood or putting kerosene in lamps. I don't know if you've ever had any of those experiences. But I think the best day in my life, the one that I remember most vividly—with the possible exception of my wedding day—was the day they turned the lights on in our house. The bringing of the rural electric program to the farms of our nation made it possible for us to stretch our hearts and stretch our minds to encompass public involvement in affairs that would not have been possible without the rural electric program."

4

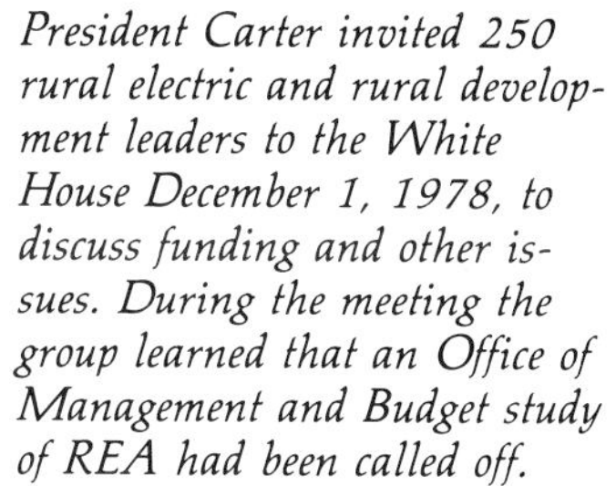

President Carter invited 250 rural electric and rural development leaders to the White House December 1, 1978, to discuss funding and other issues. During the meeting the group learned that an Office of Management and Budget study of REA had been called off.

5

Left: Vice President George Bush greeted the 1983 Rural Electric Youth Tour participants on the White House lawn. Below: During the visit, President Ronald Reagan's helicopter landed nearby, and he paused to greet the participants.

6

1

2

Below: Getting there is half the fun. W.E. Garrett and E.Z. McDuffy on special Georgia rural electric train to 1947 NRECA annual meeting in Spokane, Washington. Left: NRECA delegates register at 1949 annual meeting in New York.

President Dwight David Eisenhower addressing a packed Armory in Washington, D.C., during the 1959 NRECA annual meeting. Delegates were cool to his proposal that REA interest rates be raised.

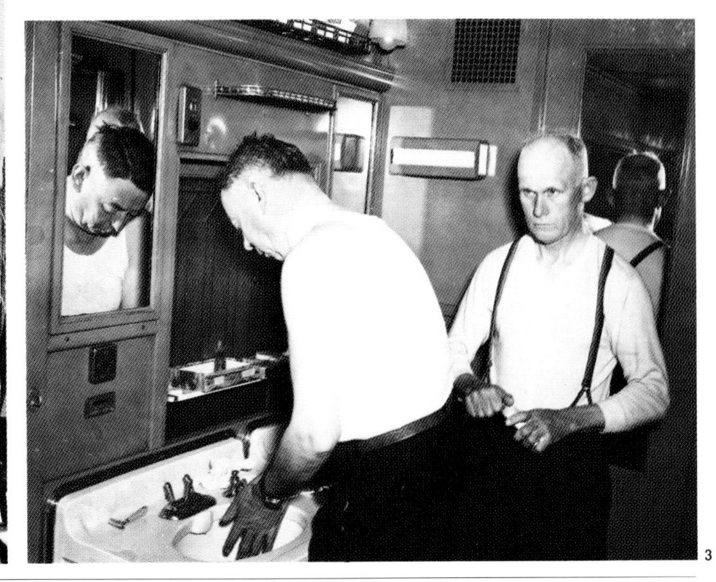

3

4

5

Above: Co-op leaders gathered in Minneapolis for an NRECA regional meeting in November, 1945, posing for this "official" picture. Those at front table, from left, are Harry Edmunds of Minnesota, an NRECA incorporator, Fred Stoneman of Wisconsin, also an incorporator and then NRECA president, and General Manager Clyde T. Ellis. Right: This scene is often repeated at NRECA annual meetings when friends spot one another. Here George Wagner, a Kelvinator representative, greeted NRECA board members Maury Williams, Alabama, and W.W. Henley, Florida, at the 1950 annual meeting in Chicago.

When Folks Get Together, Things Happen

NRECA is recognized as an organization with true grass-roots direction of its programs and activities. The way that direction is provided is perhaps unique to national associations.

In spite of the fact that state associations of rural electric cooperatives provided strong leadership in the early days of the program, their "national" did not evolve into a federation of these associations. Instead, each cooperative holds its membership directly in NRECA. Most also have membership in their state and regional service organizations.

Over the years, individual member systems of NRECA have participated in policy development in three major ways:

- Each selects a delegate (one member, one vote) to the association's annual and regional meetings.
- Each has one vote within its state for the election of a director to the NRECA board.
- Each has one vote in its region. For this purpose, NRECA has divided the nation into 10 areas with approximately the same number of rural electric systems to elect a representative to each of 13 policy-making committees in specific subject-matter areas.

1

2

Left: Wisconsin co-op leaders contemplated an agreement to distribute aluminum conductor at this meeting after World War II. Lower left: In 1953, NRECA began offering training for managers, directors and employees of rural electric cooperatives and today the program reaches more than 10,000 annually. Standing is Robert I. Kabat, director of management services for the association. Lower right: Electric co-op employee benefit programs are overseen by both a membership committee and a committee of the NRECA board of directors; this was the board committee in 1973.

3

4

Opposite page, top: An elected resolutions committee, such as this one at the 1953 NRECA annual meeting, coordinates resolutions recommended by a dozen other elected standing committees. Right: Women had an official role in the NRECA resolutions process beginning in 1964. This is the 1970 committee.

5

6

7

Above: NRECA board committee meeting in Washington, 1976. Left: Delegates registering for an NRECA regional meeting in Little Rock, Arkansas, 1944. Right: REA Administrator Harold V. Hunter responded to questions during a National Rural Electric Women's Association meeting at the 1984 annual meeting while Jo Jacobson, North Dakota, president, listened.

8

Grass-roots policy development begins at meetings of each local rural electric system. Resolutions adopted there go forward to state associations and to NRECA. Delegates at state meetings also develop policies that are passed on to NRECA committees for consideration.

Every fall a resolutions committee in each of the 10 regions considers suggestions forwarded to it, recommending policy positions accepted, rejected or amended by the delegates at the meeting. Before the fall swing of 10 regional meetings begins, the resolutions to be considered are circulated to each cooperative for study.

Resolutions adopted at each regional meeting are forwarded to the appropriate policy committee for consideration at NRECA's annual meeting early each year. Final policy decisions are made at a closing business session, based on the recommendations from the policy committees.

If all of this sounds like a lot of meetings, it's only the beginning. Almost every day somewhere in the U.S. there is a conference, workshop or seminar being conducted by NRECA for rural electric directors and employees. Operating an electric utility is a complicated and demanding business calling for continuing leadership development and advanced, specialized training.

Below: Kika de la Garza, Texas, chairman of the House Agriculture Committee, addressing the 1983 NRECA annual meeting.

Right: Former Vice President Alban Barkley was the speaker at the 1953 annual meeting of Planters Electric Membership Corporation, Georgia. Walter Harrison, NRECA Georgia director (seated, left), enjoyed it.

1

2

3

Left: Kansas Senator Robert Dole and Anne Armstrong, third from left, co-chairmen of the Republican National Committee, posed here with Barbara Deverick of Blue Ridge Electric Membership Corporation, North Carolina, and REA Administrator David A. Hamil. They spoke on a panel during the 1972 annual meeting.

4

Above: Congressman Ed Jones of Tennessee at 1981 annual meeting. Right: Secretary of State Dean Rusk, 1966.

5

6

Jerry Voorhis, president of the Cooperative League of the USA and former California Congressman, was a frequent speaker at NRECA meetings.

7

Since NRECA is also organized as a cooperative, each member system has one vote when resolutions are considered at the business session during the annual meeting. Left: Voting delegates registering for the 1967 annual meeting in San Francisco. Right: Lawrence Phelps, director of Gunnison County Electric Association, waiting for an answer to his question during the 1980 annual meeting. Below: Delegate raising a point concerning Long Range Study Committee recommendations at the 1969 annual meeting.

8

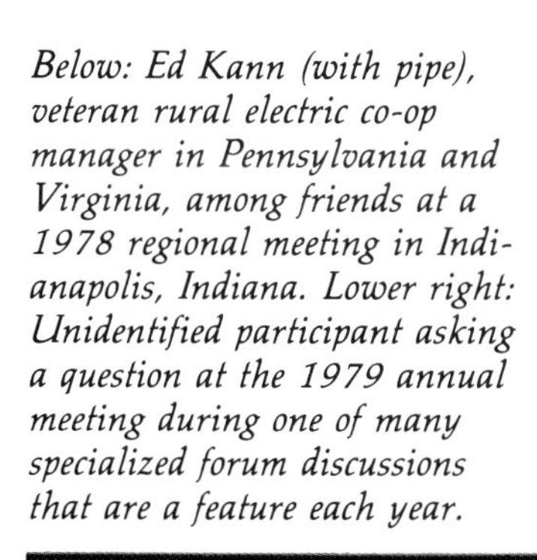

Below: Ed Kann (with pipe), veteran rural electric co-op manager in Pennsylvania and Virginia, among friends at a 1978 regional meeting in Indianapolis, Indiana. Lower right: Unidentified participant asking a question at the 1979 annual meeting during one of many specialized forum discussions that are a feature each year.

9

10

11

1

2

Annual meeting features include the latest products at the Rural Electric Expo (left), a feed put on by the Action Committee for Rural Electrification (above), press conferences with speakers such as Agriculture Secretary Clifford Hardin (middle left), and once included the Miss Rural Electrification Pageant (below).

3

4

Two features of the 1962 meeting in Atlantic City were (below) North Carolina co-op manager F.E. Joyner's chest carrying a badge from every NRECA annual meeting and (right) the "nor'easter" which wrecked the piers and marooned delegates in their hotel lobbies.

5

6

7

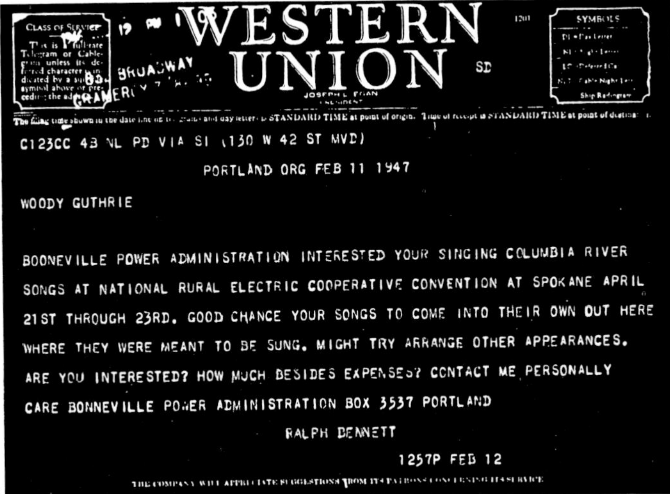

WESTERN UNION

JOSEPH L. EGAN PRESIDENT

SD

The filing time shown in the date line on telegrams and day letters is STANDARD TIME at point of origin. Time of receipt is STANDARD TIME at point of destination

C123CC 43 NL PD VIA SI (130 W 42 ST MVD)

PORTLAND ORG FEB 11 1947

WOODY GUTHRIE

BOONEVILLE POWER ADMINISTRATION INTERESTED YOUR SINGING COLUMBIA RIVER SONGS AT NATIONAL RURAL ELECTRIC COOPERATIVE CONVENTION AT SPOKANE APRIL 21ST THROUGH 23RD. GOOD CHANCE YOUR SONGS TO COME INTO THEIR OWN OUT HERE WHERE THEY WERE MEANT TO BE SUNG. MIGHT TRY ARRANGE OTHER APPEARANCES. ARE YOU INTERESTED? HOW MUCH BESIDES EXPENSES? CONTACT ME PERSONALLY CARE BONNEVILLE POWER ADMINISTRATION BOX 3537 PORTLAND

RALPH BENNETT

1257P FEB 12

8

9

Ironically, the power companies' Reddy Kilowatt (top), later an arch-rival of rural electrification's Willie Wiredhand, welcomed delegates to the 1947 NRECA meeting in Spokane, where Woody Guthrie (right) was hired by the Bonneville Power Administration (above) to sing the songs, such as "Roll On, Columbia, Roll On," which he had written for Bonneville earlier in the decade.

10

Other distinguished entertainers at NRECA annual meetings included North Dakota Senator William Langer (left), shown in this impromptu session in Atlantic City in 1955, and Graham Jackson (right) in 1949 in New York, one of several times the Georgia pianist-accordianist—a favorite of President Roosevelt—entertained at NRECA functions.

11

THIS CHECK IS IN PAYMENT OF THE FOLLOWING ACCOUNT. ENDORSEMENT BY PAYEE CONSTITUTES RECEIPT IN FULL. IF INCORRECT PLEASE RETURN

DATE	PARTICULARS	AMOUNT

24

REDDY KILOWATT, INC.
50 CHURCH STREET
NEW YORK 7, N. Y.

No. 5308

March 29, 1957. 1-2/210

PAY TO THE ORDER OF *** See Below $ 1,195.25

One Thousand One Hundred Ninety Five and 25/100 DOLLARS

REDDY KILOWATT, INC.

THE CHASE MANHATTAN BANK
214 BROADWAY
NEW YORK, N. Y.

PRESIDENT
VICE PRES. & TREASURER
VICE PRESIDENT
SECRETARY

* Payable to NRECA Patent Attorneys, names withheld upon request of those attorneys.

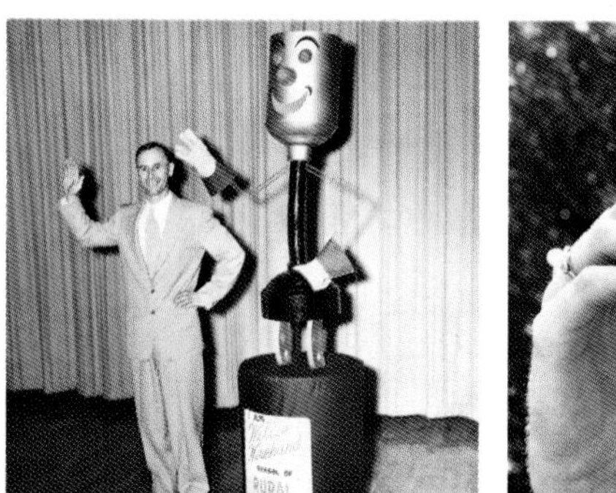

Top left: Drew McLay created Willie out of a socket and plug, some bare and insulated wire, dubbed him Willie Wiredhand, a play on the fact that wire brought farm families a new hired hand. Top right: McLay couldn't resist getting in a dig after Willie had turned back Reddy Kilowatt's court challenge in 1956. Above: Reddy's check reimbursed NRECA for some costs associated with the litigation. Middle left: Ray Howard of Jump River Electric, Wisconsin, posed with his co-op's animated version of Willie in 1954. Middle right: Willie is found on almost anything associated with rural electrification—or whatever. Left: In 1965 Willie got a first-class ride on Northeast Airlines to his new home in Washington. Bradford Warren of Boston (Willie's seatmate) built this five-foot prototype out of fiberglass, steel. Model sold for $250 and many are still greeting co-op members.

Right: Sometimes even Presidents emulated Willie: LBJ struck this Willie pose while speaking at the 1968 NRECA annual meeting in Dallas, Texas. Below: NRECA Artist Nanton Romney at Willie Wiredhand Services booth during 1964 annual meeting in Dallas. Display reveals some of the many chores Willie performed for rural electrification. Lower right: Victor Hanson, manager of Agra Lite Electric Co-op, Minnesota, presented a Willie tie to Senator Hubert Humphrey during the co-op's "Willie Wiredhand Days" in 1954.

'He's Small, But Wire-y'

Friction between rural electric co-ops and commercial power companies began to peak in the 1950s. The intensity of the battle can be seen in a court confrontation between Willie Wiredhand, symbol of rural electrification, and Reddy Kilowatt, symbol of the companies.

Reddy was the brainchild of Ashton B. Collins, an Alabama Power Company employee, in 1924. When co-ops later came on the scene, Collins refused to license them, saying Reddy was reserved for "investor-owned, tax-paying" electric utilities.

NRECA countered by developing its own symbol. A contest at its 1949 annual meeting produced an unsuccessful character named Elec Tricity. Andrew L. McLay, an entomologist turned artist and later a long-time NRECA employee, then was commissioned to create a suitable trademark. He came up with Willie.

In 1953 ownership of Reddy passed to a group of 76 power companies. Three weeks later Reddy sued a South Carolina co-op that was using Willie, charging copyright infringement.

Finally, after a week-long trial in January, 1956, a U.S. District Court ruled that Reddy couldn't have a monopoly on cartoon characters symbolizing electricity. The Court of Appeals upheld that decision on January 7, 1957.

Willie went on to become one of the best-known symbols in rural America, his profile emblazoned on office buildings, trucks, uniforms, signs, light bulbs—you name it.

Of late, fashion has decreed that cartoon symbols aren't dignified and Willie's popularity has waned. But don't count him out—even though he's past the same ripe age that Reddy was when Willie (a mere six year old) bested him in court!

1

2

3

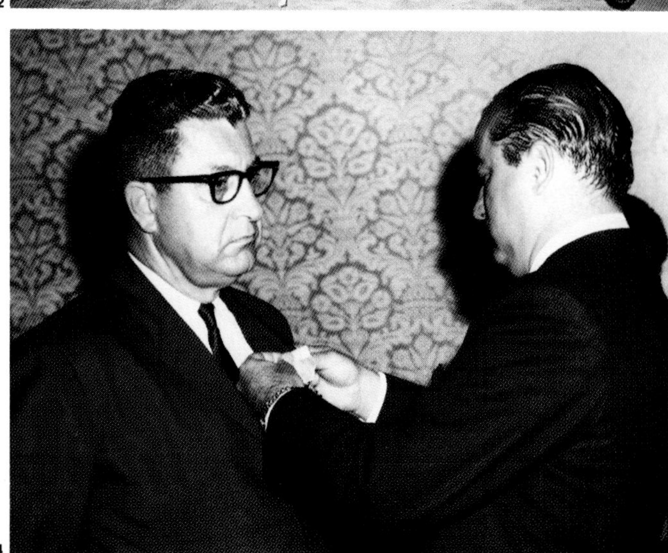
4

Above left: Wiring the home of the Florendo Mupas family on Mindoro Island, Philippines, 1983. Above: "Electro Pepe" is the name given in Latin America to Willie Wiredhand, U.S. rural electrification symbol. Left: President of Ecuador presents J.K. Smith of Kentucky the National Order of Merit. Kentucky co-ops donated equipment for a power plant (right) dedicated in Ecuador in 1967.

5

6

7

Opposite, top: Clyde Ellis signing first AID-NRECA agreement during White House ceremony, November 1, 1962. Above: Sign in Ecuador during co-op dedication. Right: Townspeople in northwest Brazil were awed when the street lights came on for the first time.

Exporting the REA Pattern

NRECA General Manager Clyde T. Ellis called it "one of the finest hours" for cooperative, self-help rural electrification. President John F. Kennedy declared, "It seems to me that the contract holds special promise for those countries which have realized only a small fraction of their energy potential."

They were commenting on an agreement between the Agency for International Development (AID) and NRECA, signed in the White House on November 1, 1962.

The agreement provided that NRECA—at the request of AID—would recruit managers, engineers and other specialists from among its member rural electric cooperatives and send them abroad for periods up to two years to help local people start their own cooperative rural electrification programs.

The AID-NRECA program became known as "exporting the REA pattern." That pattern was government assistance and training to help local, self-help cooperative electrification projects get started in much the same way that REA helped U.S. electric cooperatives get off the ground in the 1930s.

The program has been so successful that the statistics rival those of U.S. rural electrification.

By 1984 NRECA's International Programs Division had worked not only through the AID program, but through international organizations and directly with foreign governments. The nearly 300 rural electric specialists sent overseas have helped start 197 rural electric cooperatives in 15 nations. These cooperatives serve more than 3.5 million meters and an estimated 24 million people.

Left: NRECA staff sent Christmas wishes to members in 1948, the first year it occupied its building at 1303 New Hampshire Avenue. Middle left: Signing documents that led to building NRECA headquarters at 2000 Florida Avenue, N.W., in 1956. Below left: House Speaker Sam Rayburn laid the cornerstone for the building at 2000 Florida Avenue in May, 1956.

Above: The first building owned by NRECA was a former residence at 1303 New Hampshire Avenue, N.W., just a block from Dupont Circle. Below: NRECA built this building at 2000 Florida Avenue, N.W., in 1956 and occupied it through 1978.

Dupont Circle: Rich In Rural Electric History

Dupont Circle is one of the best-known areas of the Nation's Capital. It has been a popular gathering place for young people and the site of uncounted demonstrations against this or that.

But the hordes that pass through and around it each day are no doubt oblivious to the fact that it is also rich in rural electric history and that many of the decisions which set the course for the program were made within two or three blocks.

Only a block west at 2000 Massachusetts Avenue—one of the three "state avenues" that converge on the Circle—was the first home of the Rural Electrification Administration beginning in 1935. Its second home was but two blocks south at 1201 Connecticut Avenue.

NRECA, after briefly occupying rented space at 416 Fifth Street, N.W., moved in 1944 to offices at 1711 Connecticut Avenue, less than three blocks north of the Circle.

In 1948 the Association moved to a building it purchased at 1303 New Hampshire Avenue, N.W., only a block away.

The Association in 1956 constructed a building at 2000 Florida Avenue, just off Connecticut Avenue about two blocks north of the Circle.

Early in 1979, NRECA moved into its new building at 1800 Massachusetts, N.W. This building fronts on both Massachusetts and Connecticut Avenues, just south and west of Dupont Circle, as well as on 18th Street, N.W.

6

7

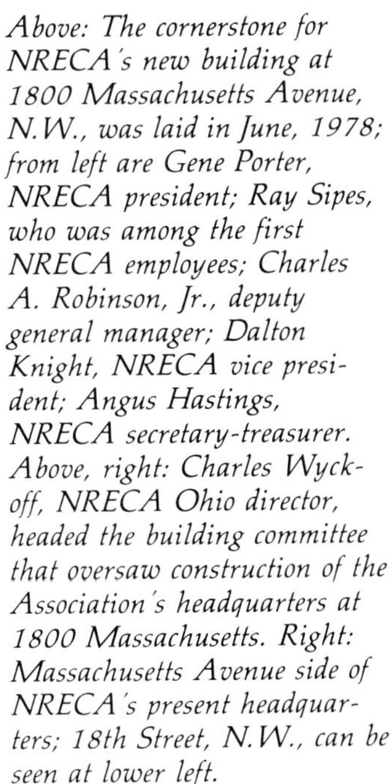

Above: The cornerstone for NRECA's new building at 1800 Massachusetts Avenue, N.W., was laid in June, 1978; from left are Gene Porter, NRECA president; Ray Sipes, who was among the first NRECA employees; Charles A. Robinson, Jr., deputy general manager; Dalton Knight, NRECA vice president; Angus Hastings, NRECA secretary-treasurer. Above, right: Charles Wyckoff, NRECA Ohio director, headed the building committee that oversaw construction of the Association's headquarters at 1800 Massachusetts. Right: Massachusetts Avenue side of NRECA's present headquarters; 18th Street, N.W., can be seen at lower left.

8

1

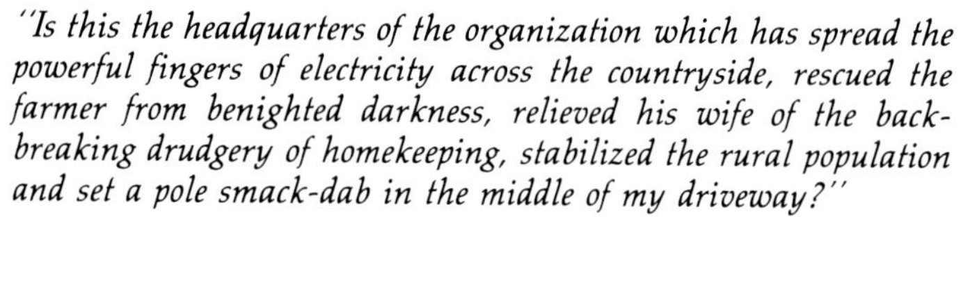

"Is this the headquarters of the organization which has spread the powerful fingers of electricity across the countryside, rescued the farmer from benighted darkness, relieved his wife of the back-breaking drudgery of homekeeping, stabilized the rural population and set a pole smack-dab in the middle of my driveway?"

2

"Remember the old days when somebody would send us a post-card saying his lights had been off a week or 10 days, and he thought maybe we'd like to know?"

3

"I still remember how her grandma cried with joy the day we hooked them up."

4

"He wants to speak to the rob-ber baron—is that you?"

5

"Miss LaDish, my reference to Director Bluff as an 'obstreper-ous old boar' was merely a par-enthetical expression that I had not intended to be included in this letter."

6

"That pole that's been setting smack-dab in the middle of my driveway the past 30 years . . . remember? Well, about 15 min-utes ago it jumped out in front of my wife while she was aiming for the garage."

'Is This the Headquarters of . . . ?'

The "cartoonist laureate" of rural electrification has always been Web Allison, a longtime employee of San Luis Valley Rural Electric Cooperative in Colorado.

His first offerings appeared in his co-op's newsletter, but for years his distinctive style has been a regular feature in publications of NRECA and the consumer publications of rural electric statewide organizations.

Web's fertile mind created PDQ Electric Co-

7

operative and peopled it with characters so human that almost anyone in rural electrification will swear he knows exactly who Web had in mind when he first drew them.

Manager Tom Boom, Director Bluff, receptionist/clerk Angie Fizzlewhite, accountant Clarence Pennyworth, McFoogle the lineman and Miss LaDish the secretary—all serve as a reminder that co-op employees and co-op members are, after all, only human.

And his gentle poking of fun at everyone from the beset manager to the confused consumer has helped keep those connected with rural electrification from taking themselves too seriously.

Web's classic cartoon encaptioned "Is this the headquarters of . . ." (reprinted opposite at top) was placed in the cornerstone of the first headquarters building NRECA constructed in 1957 and was later transferred to the cornerstone of the Association's present headquarters at 1800 Massachusetts Avenue in Washington in 1979.

8

"Remember when we'd vote to buy a new set of tires for the service truck, settle on the entertainment for the annual meeting and figure we'd put in a full day?"

9

"Mama said you got electricity here right after the war. Was that the Civil War?"

Above: The Long-Range Study Committee, established by NRECA to examine financial needs and program objectives, held the first of 32 meetings in Washington in November, 1967.

Right: The first Governor of CFC, J.K. Smith, headed the NRECA study committee that recommended its creation.

Left: Charles Gill was named the second Governor of CFC in September, 1979. Seen here with David Hamil.

"All right, then, what would you call it?"

One of the knotty problems faced by the Long-Range Study Committee was what to name its new creation. The answer was to name it the National Rural Utilities Cooperative Finance Corporation—and call it "CFC." Above: Cartoonist Web Allison takes note of the committee's predicament. CFC's headquarters in Washington is located in Georgetown; shown at left is the J.K. Smith Building when it was dedicated early in 1979.

6

Above: First board of directors of CFC in 1969 or 1970; outside of table, from left: Sailey Ennis, Virgil Herriott, Robert D. Partridge, John Pierce, T.W. Hunter, Leland Leatherman, J.K. Smith, Vince Slatt, Earl King, Raymond W. Rusteberg, James R. Cobb, Leland Kitt; inside table: Tim Dudley, William Carleton, E.V. Lewis, Lloyd Patton, Clarence Peterson, Walter Harrison.

7

Left: REA Administrator David A. Hamil and CFC Governor J.K. Smith announce the first concurrent loan at the NRECA Annual Meeting in Dallas, Texas, February 16, 1971.

Looking at the Long Range

Since 1935 the rural electric cooperatives had depended exclusively upon loans from REA to meet their capital requirements. In the late 1950s when the interest rate on government borrowings rose significantly higher than the two percent rate that REA had been charging since 1944, pressures began to mount for the rural electrics to provide for their own needs.

A study by a New York financial firm produced a recommendation in the early 1960s that a Rural Electric Bank, patterned after the Bank for Cooperatives, be established. But after the failure of both the 89th and 90th Congresses to approve such a bank, co-op leaders sought a new approach.

In 1967 the NRECA members established a blue-ribbon "Long-Range Study Committee" to make a comprehensive review of the entire rural electrification program, identifying and defining goals and objectives, and, after evaluation, to bring forth recommendations.

The panel of 26 rural electric leaders began its work in November, 1967, and spent the next 16 months listening to local leaders and national figures and studying and planning before making its final recommendations at the 1969 NRECA annual meeting. One recommendation called for the creation of a self-help, independent organization to provide financing to supplement that available through REA.

Based on the plan developed by the committee, the National Rural Utilities Cooperative Finance Corporation—commonly called "CFC"—was incorporated in April, 1969. Since then CFC has loaned more than $3 billion in long-term capital to its member rural electric systems. In addition it has guaranteed more than $4 billion in loans for pollution control equipment and provides its members with ready access to $2.5 billion in short-term credit.

Left: The first three administrators of REA gathered in Washington when Harry Slattery (center) was sworn in on September 26, 1939; at left is first administrator, Morris L. Cooke, and right is second, John Carmody. Below: REA Administrator Claude Wickard (left) and Vermont Senator George Aiken (right) were speakers at Washington Electric Co-op (Vermont) and Vermont Electric Co-op in the fall of 1946. Here they are shown with Vermont EC manager Harry D. Bowman at the co-op headquarters.

When the Secretary of Agriculture or the REA administrator was a farmer, USDA and REA publicists liked to have photos taken "back home." Left: Administrator Claude Wickard on his Carroll County, Indiana, farm in 1942 when he was Secretary of Agriculture. Right: Administrator Ancher Nelsen on his Minnesota farm in 1953.

5

6

7

The REA administrator has always been a welcome speaker at annual and regional meetings of NRECA. Above left: Ancher Nelsen addressing NRECA's annual meeting, probably in 1956. Above: David A. Hamil being sworn in for his first term as REA administrator on June 26, 1956. Left: In keeping with the tradition of showing administrators back on the farm, this photo has David A. Hamil surveying part of the 3,000 head of cattle he and his brother Donald raised on their 3,000-acre Colorado ranch in the summer of 1956.

REA Administrators: Profiles of Leadership

Out of necessity, REA turned to cooperatives in 1935 as the tool for getting electricity to rural areas. As it nurtured the new co-ops, a close relationship developed between the "banker" and the "borrower," a relationship probably unrivaled by any other agency.

Every administrator from Morris L. Cooke on down made a practice of getting out among REA's borrowers, finding out their needs and then directing the agency to respond promptly. And administrators haven't been bashful about prodding and pushing—even ordering—them to adopt certain management practices.

Because of this close relationship, and because of the knowledge of what the agency has meant to them and their neighbors, local co-op leaders have always had a special feeling of respect for the office of administrator.

Since Cooke was named administrator of REA in 1935, only eight others have held the post:

John M. Carmody (1937-1939); Harry Slattery (1939-1944); Claude R. Wickard (1945-1953); Ancher Nelsen (1953-1956); David A. Hamil (1956-1961 and 1969-1978); Norman M. Clapp (1961-1969); Robert W. Feragen (1978-1981); Harold Hunter (1981-).

Four have been farmers (Wickard, Nelsen, Hamil and Hunter), two were engineers (Cooke and Carmody), one was an editor (Clapp), one a career rural electric employee, primarily in communications and management (Feragen), and one a career government manager (Slattery).

Right: REA Administrator Norman M. Clapp addressing the annual meeting of NRECA in 1968. Below: Clapp tried out a hand-cranked magneto telephone on April 25, 1967, as Edgar F. Renshaw, assistant administrator-telephone, watched; the phone was in service in an Arkansas farmhouse for 40 years and was one of the last crank phones in the state.

Above: When Clapp threw the switch at the John McGuffin ranch near Tatum, New Mexico, on July 2, 1962, it turned on the power to the five-millionth REA consumer; Lea County Electric Co-op manager R.B. Moore is at Clapp's right. Left: Clapp (left) and Moore (center) presented Secretary of Agriculture Orville Freeman with the McGuffins' kerosene lamp.

Right: On May 10, 1962, Clapp approved a $36,000,000 loan to Basin Electric Power Cooperative, the first step in building the large North Dakota-based generation and transmission system. South Dakotans at the signing, from left, were: Dail Gibbs, manager, South Dakota Rural Electric Association; Arthur Jones, president, Basin Electric; Otto Schneider, president, Moreau Grand Electric Co-op; Virgil T. Hanlon, manager, East River Power Cooperative; L.H. Jacobson, manager, Rushmore Electric Power Cooperative; A.C. Hauffe, president, South Dakota Rural Electric Association.

Right: On August 20, 1974, REA and the Federal Financing Bank signed an agreement providing for FFB to make loans guaranteed by REA; from left, Will Erwin, assistant secretary of agriculture for rural development; Jack A. Bennett, center, president of the Federal Financing Bank; REA Administrator David A. Hamil. Middle right: Rural Electric Youth Tour participants presented Dave Hamil with this autographed drawing of himself in recognition of his total of ten years as REA Administrator in June, 1974.

6

7

8

9

Middle left: Hamil, seated, signed a loan guarantee commitment of $513 million to Oglethorpe EMC, Georgia, on January 10, 1975. Funds were used to purchase a 30 percent share of two Georgia Power Company plants; others from left: Walter Harrison, executive vice president of Georgia EMC; J. Phil Campbell, agriculture under secretary; I.F. Murph, Oglethorpe president; James E. Bostic, assistant secretary of agriculture; Edwin I. Hatch, president, Georgia Power Company. Left: Hamil at work in his office near the beginning of his second term as REA Administrator. Right: Hamil addressing 1978 NRECA annual meeting.

10

1

REA Administrator Robert W. Feragen addressing the 1980 annual meeting of NRECA. Right: David A. Hamil congratulating his successor after Feragen was sworn in at the Department of Agriculture. Below: Mrs. Feragen watched as her husband was sworn in by Secretary of Agriculture Bob Bergland, October 30, 1978, as the eighth individual to be REA Administrator.

2

3

4

Middle right: Feragen discussing issues with a reporter in 1979. Right: Feragen addressed a group of rural electric leaders at the White House, December 1, 1978, before an appearance by President Carter.

5

6

Left: Administrator Harold V. Hunter on his ranch in Oklahoma. Right: Hunter addressing 1983 NRECA annual meeting. Below: Top REA electric staff in 1984, from left: Joe Zoller, assistant administrator; William Davis, western director; Frank Bennett, north central director; Archie Cain, engineering standards director; Donald L. Olsen, deputy to Zoller; Thomas B. Heath, southwest director; Martin G. Seipel, northeast director; Joseph R. Binder, southeast director.

7

Below: Hunter meeting with his top staff in 1984, from left: Blaine Stockton, Jr., assistant administrator-management; Hunter; Joe Zoller, assistant administrator-electric; John Arnesen, assistant administrator-telephone; Jack Van Mark, deputy administrator.

8

9

10

11

Above: Hunter being sworn in by Deputy Secretary of Agriculture Richard E. Lyng, August 6, 1981. Left: The terms of these four REA administrators reach back to 1956. They were photographed together while attending an NRECA regional meeting in Rapid City, South Dakota, in 1981; from left: Norman M. Clapp, David A. Hamil, Harold V. Hunter, Robert W. Feragen.

Right: Robert D. Partridge succeeded Clyde T. Ellis as executive vice president and general manager of NRECA in February, 1968.

1

2

Above: Partridge (second from right) enjoying a comment by Vice President Hubert Humphrey at meeting of NRECA's Long-Range Study Committee in 1968. Left: Besides being general manager, he was also a major general, having served in WW II and Korea, and was the U.S. Army's highest-ranking reserve officer in 1973. Lower left: Partridge, shown kicking off a Co-op Month meeting at the State Department, was active with many other cooperative organizations. Below: Partridge, often a witness at key Congressional hearings where he was noted for presenting his case factually and forthrightly, testifying on REA appropriations before Florida Senator Spessard Holland.

3

5

4

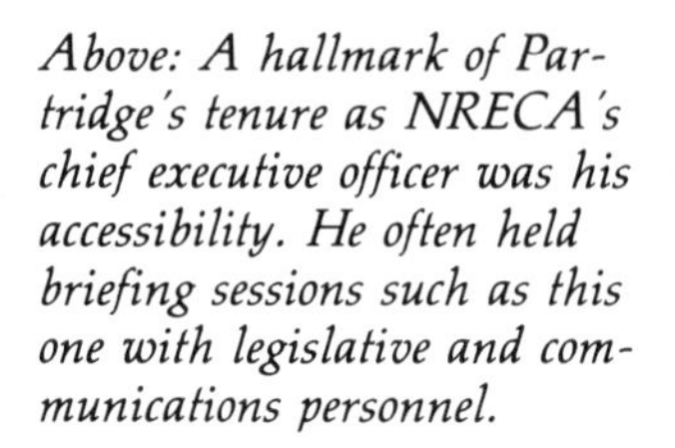

Above: A hallmark of Partridge's tenure as NRECA's chief executive officer was his accessibility. He often held briefing sessions such as this one with legislative and communications personnel.

7

Above: Partridge and his wife, Georgiann, at his retirement dinner in Washington, March, 1984.

6

8

Left: Bob Bergland, former Congressman and U.S. Secretary of Agriculture, became the third head of NRECA in April, 1984.

Below: The hometown folks in Minnesota celebrate their favorite son.

9

10

11

Middle above: Bergland and NRECA President Guy C. Lewis of Virginia listening to reports during a meeting of the NRECA board of directors. Above: Bergland at his desk in NRECA's headquarters in Washington.

'Men of the Land'

The NRECA board chose another man with his roots in the land to succeed Clyde Ellis. Robert D. Partridge, a native of rural Missouri who had joined the NRECA staff in 1961 following a career as a key staff member of REA, became general manager in 1968.

His first two years saw a comprehensive review of program objectives and financing alternatives culminate in the formation of a self-help financing cooperative. "Black Friday" came only months after that organization made its first loan. Partridge led a successful mobilization to overturn the termination of the REA lending program.

Partridge's 16 years as head of the association were marked by increasing cohesiveness of the members and steady growth to meet NRECA members' needs for additional services.

When Partridge announced his retirement, the choice for his replacement was another "man of the land": Bob Bergland, a farmer, former Congressman and U.S. Secretary of Agriculture. He began operating as head of NRECA in April, 1984, and brought with him the additional credentials of having been an executive with the nation's largest farmer co-op—and the son of an organizer of an electric co-op.

Because There *Is* Electricity

Rural America today. Vast and changing. Providing high-quality food and fiber for the nation and the world. Room for commercial and industrial growth. A new-found home for crowd-weary people.

Because there ***is*** electricity.

Because there ***is*** electricity, the American farmer and rancher has been able to increase his productivity to easily feed our nation and to help feed a hungry world—at a cost that allows Americans to spend less of their income for food than people of any other nation in the world.

Because there ***is*** electricity, millions of acres of otherwise arid or marginal farmland can be irrigated, stabilizing food production and lessening potential perils of drought and famine.

Because there ***is*** electricity, Americans eat fresh foods of a quality that defies comparison with those of just a generation ago.

Because there ***is*** electricity, small industries—or large ones—can locate in rural areas, providing jobs for the people there, diminishing population pressures on America's cities.

Because there ***is*** electricity, millions of Americans have a real choice about where and how they want to live.

Rural America today: a place where native sons and daughters are returning with families . . . to jobs, to services and opportunities once only dreams.

Rural America, a land of opportunity, still.

Because there is electricity.

Opposite page: Big Cajun No. 2 generating station of Cajun Electric Power Cooperative, New Roads, Louisiana, provides power for rural electric systems across the state.

Above: Although consolidations have closed most one- and two-room rural schools, some still exist. Here children are raising the flag at the electrified District 167 School, Cherry County, Nebraska.

Above: Electrically heated hog facilities mean greater efficiency and more profit to farmers. Left: The "big top" annual meeting still exists in Kentucky and draws crowds such as this one at South Kentucky Rural Electric Cooperative Corporation in Somerset. Below: Marion and Earl Baker enjoy rural living—with electricity—near Hillsboro, Virginia.

Today, most co-ops provide advice on energy use and conservation. At left, Member Services Advisor Sammie Derickson of Niobrara Valley Rural Electric Co-op checking rain gauge with member Elmer Bore near O'Neill, Nebraska.

6

Tammy Wolfenden studying in a well-lighted rural school in Cherry County, Nebraska. Right: With or without electricity, feeding the calves is still a farm chore for the youngsters. Below: The Doug Higgins family of Idaho County, Idaho, is among the "new wave" of rural Americans who prefer living in the country, but who worry about the number of people flocking to their area.

7

9

Many co-op annual meetings are still held with the same excitement as during the first 20 years of rural electrification. Right: Chowing down at the annual meeting of Verendrye Electric Cooperative, North Dakota. Below: Crowd at Inter-County Rural Electric Cooperative Corporation meeting in Kentucky.

8

10

Even though the pastoral scenes at right and in the lower right might indicate otherwise, farming is vastly different today because there is electricity. The quantity of today's food and its quality defy comparison with a generation ago.

1

2

3

The difference electricity makes can be seen in this hog confinement farm at left and in the grain delivery system above, both in Holt County, Nebraska.

4

5

Electricity is an essential ingredient in today's poultry and egg operations. Automatic equipment and heating ensure that products which reach market are fresh and of high quality.

6

7

8

Above: Because there is electricity, millions of acres of otherwise arid or marginal farmland can be irrigated, stabilizing food production, lessening potential perils of drought and famine. This irrigation operation is in the San Luis Valley, Alamosa County, Colorado. Left: Some things, like roping calves, are still done the "old-fashioned way."

Because there is electricity, businesses can locate in rural areas where there is a good labor supply. Right: The Galleria, served by Cobb Electric Membership Corporation, Marietta, Georgia. Below: A citrus nursery in Wachula, Florida. Lower left: A rural factory at Logan, Ohio. Lower right: An oil rig in North Dakota.

1

2

3

4

5

6

7

8

Upper left: Making window frames near Warroad, Minnesota. Upper right: Union REC serves the new Honda automobile plant near Marysville, Ohio. Above: Patuxent Naval Air Station in Maryland is one of many defense installations served by rural electric cooperatives. Left: Closed-loop heat pumps provide economical cooling and heating and are becoming popular installations in rural areas, such as this one near Hamilton, Ohio.

Above: Extra-high voltage transmission lines are maintained and operated regionally by Basin Electric Power Cooperative to deliver wholesale power to its member distribution co-ops in eight states.

Right: An environmental technician of Hoosier Energy Corp. of Indiana inspects sulfur dioxide "scrubber" system on Merom generating station, Sullivan, Indiana. Below: The 450,000 kilowatt Coleman plant of Big Rivers Electric Corp., Hawesville, Kentucky, is reflected in waters of Ohio River at dusk.

4

Left: Power from Coal Creek plant in North Dakota, owned by United and Cooperative Power Associations, Minnesota G&Ts, is carried to giant converter at Buffalo, MN (below), and changed from direct to alternating current for delivery to co-ops.

5

6

7

Left: Overhaul time at Leland Olds plant of Basin Electric, Stanton, North Dakota.

Above: REA symbol glows brightly at rural electric office of Niobrara Valley EMC in Nebraska.

1

2

3

A Celebration of Success

by Robert W. Feragen

I

Take time to celebrate,
Having caution for what is true
Of times past and people of the land.
Take care, as if in prayer, to mark well our passage
Across half a century of America's brightened way.

Hard won, our country lights are beautiful with prospect,
Reality surpassing the dream.
Our achievement greater than our strength:
Not the glory of light alone,
But the radiance of minds and souls,
And the promise and power of hope.

Dreamers became catalyst to our dreams.
We told ourselves it was not possible to do this.
Roosevelt-crazy, Norris-tomfoolery,
The Texas politics of Sam Rayburn.
Yet it was what they knew and we knew:
Respect for its rural people, all its people,
Frees the Republic from old Europe's bonds.
Faith in what we could do together
Excited hope everywhere in the land.
The Rural Electrification Administration,
Became familiar as "The REA,"
Its best years and best people
Magnified what was capable among us.
Together we created anew the spirit of rural community,
The giving more respected than gain,
Our joining hands signifying a greater hope.

II

The foolishness began with the sign-up:
A Dirty Thirties certainty
That the five dollars would come to naught.
Yet we were strong enough to take the chance,
Proud enough to hope again for ourselves,
Weary enough to crave better for our children.
So, we decided to try the REA, risk five bucks.

GRAND GR RY CO.
QUALITY MEATS
GROCERIE
NEW
POTATOES
6 LB 23
NEW
LARGE
POTATOES
6 LB 23
APPLES
DELICIOUS
4 LB 25
ORANGES
1¢
GRAPEFRUIT
5¢
BETTER LOAF
UNION LEADER
PIPE OR CIGARETTE
PEPSI-COLA 5¢
7up
IT LIKES YOU
RICE KRISPIES
BEECH-NUT
CHEWING TOBACCO
Chew Copenhagen
It's a pleasure
Did you say 10¢?
MODEL
SMOKING TOBACCO

1

2

WOLFE COUNTY OFFICE
WPA
PROJECT SUPERINTENDENT

3

You say, that's not so much to chance,
But all the eggs we gathered in a hot July week
Would not bring five whole dollars at the store.
A man could work four, maybe five days for cash money
Counted out to five whole dollars.
It was like throwing away two pairs of new overalls,
A bandana and a tobacco plug thrown in,
To sign up a five dollar membership for light.

But, "What the hell," we said,
The missus would like some nice things,
Company of radio music, an iron heated by electricity.
Those were the thoughts that turned our minds,
Knowing we lived simple and our women dressed plain.
But we remembered the smile of youth,
The hope we had together for the soil.
And the women, for their part more shrewd,
Always cautious of promises too large, hope too easy,
Yet eyes bright for value in dreams,
Dug into egg money for the five-dollar gamble.
Another concession made; cherished things put off again.
What we all knew was that we were no peasant race,
Left behind in old Europe.
Our promise was greater.

We began to see a country landscape of purpose,
A wide rural expanse made bright for a free people.
So we signed up; power in that alone.
Think of the miraculous unfolding,
Even before the lights.
Think of the spirit of those who rode country miles,
Talking neighbor talk to get around to the five dollars,
Try to feel how embarrassed one can be,
Asking for money of a man who doesn't have it,
Asking for hope he gave up yesterday.
Our eyes were upon each other for signals,
Signs of anger or despair.
No easy emotions come to men and women
Unrewarded for labor honestly sweated.
We watched each other.
We wondered if it might happen to us:
A liberation.

III

We became determined upon our landscape of purpose,
Found in cooperation our single strength to survive.

1

2

3

Our histories are all different; all the same.
Wire unreeled, poles set in hand-dug holes,
Prairie soil or Allegheny hills,
Bayou swamp, or Rocky Mountain passes
Made way for new lines among our lives.
We set them right, first the poles and then the scoffers.
When the people say "yes" to themselves
The countryside blossoms with bright purpose.
Whether forgotten and learned again,
The centuries taught us not to want too much.
In those days of growing hope throughout the land,
We learned to nurture light hearts.
We took time to sit upon the barn roof
To watch fox pups play in our field.
We climbed the ridge of a prairie hill
Searching for wild berries in the fall,
Where cockleburrs and spear grass made the getting harder,
Certifying the value of our adventure.
Deep within a southern woods,
Father and son sat listening to the hound's sweet song,
Pretty as any boy could imagine.
Ranch hands trailing homeward in winter
Marvelled at the winking distant stars.

What was built is not for us alone,
Nor for our children only.
The legacy is the future we make possible:
Cooperation arising from each community,
Built upon the democratic dream.
From rural electrification for and by the people
Comes a gift to all the nation:
A landscape peopled for freedom,
Rural America binding all America.
Weigh the prize by no balance sheet
But in the heart.

We celebrate the success of many hands.
Listen to the song of our common voice,
New lines whispering on prairie winds,
Whistling on the Outer Banks
Carolling the rich land
Like a surprising hymn,
The doxology of our faith in each other.

NOTES AND CREDITS

ACKNOWLEDGMENTS

We want to particularly thank the following individuals for their help in finding and supplying us photographs:

James C. Anderson, director, Photographic Archives, Eckstrom Library, University of Louisville, Louisville, KY

Merritt E. Bailey, director of book publishing, Iowa State University Press, Ames

Deborah Bouton, editor, *Rural America,* Rural America, Inc., Washington, DC

Leroy Bellamy, reference librarian, Prints and Photographs Division, Library of Congress

Susan Bosanko and **Mark Renovitch,** archivists, Franklin D. Roosevelt Library, Hyde Park, NY

Richard Crawford, archivist of the REA documentary records, Scientific, Economic & Natural Resources Branch, the National Archives

Cynthia Ghee, supervisor of the Central Research Room, and her staff, the National Archives

Betty Hill, archivist, and **Deborah Edge,** archives technician, Still Pictures Branch, the National Archives

Kathrine Hourigan, Alfred A. Knopf, New York, NY

Irlene Lewis Hess, former REA employee who provided photos of REA's St. Louis years, Accokeek, MD

Ian McLeod, senior editor, Power Information Staff, TVA, Chattanooga, TN

Jean Mosley, visual information specialist, Public Information Office, REA

Terry Olbrysh, director of public relations, ALCAN Aluminum Corporation, Cleveland, OH

Cora Lee Paull, photo researcher, St. Louis, MO

Bill Reade, pioneer REA employee who traveled with the first "REA Circus," now retired in IA

Stephanie Smith and her colleagues, Photocomposition Services, U.S. News & World Report, for the excellent typography

Dorothy Staats, photo researcher, Photography Center, Office of Government and Public Affairs, USDA

Gene Tollefson, BPA, Portland, OR

Ann Wallmark, correspondence clerk, Photo Duplication Service, Library of Congress

Thomas M. Whitehead and **George Brightbill,** Samuel Paley Library, Temple University

Dan Yearout, photographer, Information Office, TVA, Knoxville, TN

Information About Notes and Credits

Every effort has been made to accurately identify each photo in this publication. In many cases, however, it was impossible. This is particularly true for pictures in the Rural Electrification Administration collection in the National Archives and those in the files of the National Rural Electric Cooperative Association.

The REA collection of negatives covers the years 1935-1962 and most of the negative jackets contain no information.

NRECA photos, most of them from the files of *Rural Electrification* magazine, often were filed with no identifying marks after use.

The credit listings which follow provide the following, when known: **(1)** *numbers of photos* as they appear on each double-page spread, **(2)** the *source of the photograph* along with *the source's negative or file number* (this is the place to order a copy of the photo), **(3)** *name of the photographer,* if known (in italics), and **(4)** *other pertinent information.*

Addresses of organizations which supplied several photographs are given in this explanatory section; otherwise the address is given within the credit.

Photos identified as "NRECA" or which contain the notation "(NRECA)" within the credit may be obtained by writing NRECA. *Please include the page and photo number* (e.g., 14-1).

National Archives photos with the prefix designation "221-G" are from the REA negative collection.

Library of Congress photos with the prefix "USF" are from the Farm Security Administration collection; those with the prefix "USW" are from the Office of War Information collection. (Photographers with the Farm Security Administration were assigned to the Office of War information at the outbreak of World War II.)

National Archives photos, Library of Congress photos and U.S. Department of Agriculture photos may be obtained directly from those organizations. Some of the REA photographs in the National Archives collection are more readily available through USDA and a few from NRECA; these are indicated within the credit.

Photos from photo services, libraries or historical societies must be ordered from them and may not be reproduced without permission of the owner.

ABBREVIATIONS AND ADDRESSES

Abbreviations used in the credits, along with the addresses of these sources:

BPA Bonneville Power Administration
(all BPA photos may be ordered from NRECA)

FDR Franklin Delano Roosevelt Library
259 Albany Post Road
Hyde Park, NY 12538

ISU Iowa State University Press
Ames, IA 50010

LC Library of Congress
Photoduplication Service
Washington, DC 20540

NA The National Archives
Still Pictures Branch
Washington, DC 20408

NRECA National Rural Electric Cooperative Association
50th Anniversary Photos
1800 Mass. Ave., NW
Washington, DC 20036

REA Public Information Office
Rural Electrification Administration
Washington, DC 20250

SONJ Standard Oil of New Jersey Collection
Photographic Archives
Eckstrom Library
University of Louisville
Louisville, KY 40292

TVA Tennessee Valley Authority
(TVA photos may be ordered through NRECA)

USDA U.S. Department of Agriculture
Photography Center
Office of Governmental and Public Affairs
Washington, DC 20250

OTHER ADDRESSES

The Bettmann Archive, Inc., 136 East 57th St., New York, NY 10022 (handles United Press International photos)

Wide World Photos, Inc., 50 Rockefeller Plaza, New York, NY 10020 (handles Associated Press photos)

PHOTO CREDITS

Pages 2-3: TVA K-1663 (NRECA).

Pages 10-11: **1** U.S. Naval Observatory M42-Orion Nebula; Flagstaff Station, P.O. Box 1149, Flagstaff, AZ 86001 (NRECA). **2** National Aeronautics and Space Administration 71-H-1435; *Apollo 15, 1971* (NRECA). **3** NRECA, Electric Power Research Institute. **4** USDA, U.S. Forest Service 499494, *Leland J. Prater* (NRECA).

Page 12: LC USF33-4048-M5, *Theodor Jung;* Brown County, IN, Oct., 1935.

Pages 14-15: **1** USDA (NRECA). **2** State Historical Society of Wisconsin WHi(X3)13454, *Martin*; Rogers Farm, Hinsdale, IL, 1927; International Harvester Collection; 816 State St., Madison, WI 53706. **3** USDA (NRECA). **4** NA 221-G-7876. **5** NA 33-SC-21647, *W.H. Conant*; Oxford, ME, Jul., 1936.

Pages 16-17: **1** USDA BN-44739. **2** LC USDA Cen-438; Wilson, MD, 1935-40. **3** State Historical Society of Wisconsin IH-29653; 816 State St., Madison, WI 53706.

Pages 18-19: **1** LC USF34-19735-E, *Dorothea Lange*; Person County, NC, Jul., 1939. **2** NA 33-S-9708. **3** NRECA, Buffalo REC. **4** NA 33-S-9708.

Pages 20-21: **1** TVA H-10 (NRECA); Mrs. Sarah J. Wilson, Bulls Gap, TN, Oct. 22, 1933. **2** USDA BN-39063, *G.W. Ackerman*; Oklahoma, Jul., 1935. **3** NA SC-18027; Granville County, NC, Sep., 1933. **4** USDA BN-44633; Haskill County, TX, 1931. **5** LC USZ62-11016, *C.H. Currier*; circa 1890s. **6** USDA 15114-C (NRECA). **7** NA 33-SC-6021. **8** NA 33-SC-7320.

Pages 22-23: **1** USDA BN-39059, *G.W. Ackerman*; Adkins Home Demonstration Club, Pope County, AR. **2** SONJ 45815, *Sol Libsohn*. **3** NA 33-SC-5825. **4** NA 33-SC-11180.

Pages 24-25: **1** LC USF33-11924-M2, *Russell Lee*; Transylvania, LA, Jan., 1939. **2** USDA BN-28896. **3** NA 33-SC-5816. **4** NA 33-SC-2890. **5** LC USF34-6819-D, *Carl M. Mydans*; Clemson, SC, Jun., 1936. **6** & **7** NRECA.

Pages 26-27: **1** USDA-REA (NRECA); Mrs. Parkinson, Belmont Co., OH. **2** LC USF34-15766-D, *Cox*; Florence County, SC, summer, 1938. **3** NA 33-S-7179. **4** TVA H-18, *Lewis Hine* (NRECA); Stooksberry homestead, Andersonville, TN, Oct. 23, 1933. **5** LC USF34-33591-D, *Russell Lee*; Sallisaw, OK, June., 1939.

Pages 28-29: **1** LC USF34-80102-D, *John Collier*; St. Mary's County, MD, Jul., 1941. **2** LC USF33-11532-M2, *Russell Lee*; New Madrid County, MO, May, 1938. **3** NA 221-G-464. **4** USDA BN-18172-X; Winchester, VA, Nov., 6, 1919. **5** LC USF34-33526, *Russell Lee*. **6** ISU, *In No Time At All*, by Carl Hamilton, 1974 (from *Farm Town, A Memoir of the 1930s*).

Pages 30-31: **1** ISU, *In No Time at All* (from LC). **2** NRECA. **3** USDA BN-44258; Winchester, VA, probably 1919. **4** LC USF33-11609-M3, *Russell Lee*; Caruthersville, MO, Aug., 1938.

Pages 32-33: **1** NA 221-G-421. **2** NA 221-G-634. **3** NA 221-G-7881. **4** LC USF33-30718-M5, *Marion Post Wolcott*; Stem, NC, Nov., 1939. **5** NA 221-G-450.

Pages 34-35: **1** NA 33-SC-15754, **2** SONJ 30910, *Esther Bubley*; newlyweds, west Texas sheep ranch, 1945. **3** USDA BN-35848. **4** LC USF34-372-D, *Arthur Rothstein*; Postmaster Brown, Old Rag, VA, Oct., 1935. **5** USDA BN-44665.

Pages 36-37: **1** NA 221-G-555. **2** NA 221-G-556. **3** LC USF342-8133A, *Walker Evans*; Floyd Burroughs home, Hale County, AL, summer 1936. **4** LC USF34-37804-D, *Russell Lee*; Pie Town, NM, Oct., 1940.

Page 38: The Bettmann Archive.

Pages 40-41: **1** LC USZ62-10650. **2** John M. Olin Library, Department of Manuscripts and University Archives N1157; Cornell University, Ithaca, NY 14853. **3** Cornell N1155. **4** NA 165-WW-438A1. **5** Iowa State Historical Society, 402 Iowa Ave., Iowa City, IA 52240. **6** From *With Horace Plunkett in Ireland*, by R.A. Anderson, Macmillan and Co., Ltd., London, 1935 (NRECA).

Pages 42-43: **1** City Archives of Philadelphia, 160 City Hall, Philadelphia, PA 19107. **2** Photojournalism Collection, Temple University Libraries, Philadelphia, PA 19122; circa Nov. 23, 1933. **3-6** *Giant Power: The Report of the Giant Power Survey*, Commonwealth of Pennsylvania, Harrisburg, 1925 (NRECA).

Pages 44-45: **1** FDR NPx-38(22); owner Wide World Photos. **2** FDR NPx51-115:-109(3), *J.T. Holloway*. **3** Temple University Libraries, *Inquirer* Photograph Collection, Philadelphia, PA 19122; owner Wide World Photos; used *Philadelphia Evening Bulletin*, Jun. 2, 1931. **4** FDR NPx51-115:109(6), *J.T. Holloway*.

Pages 46-47: **1** LC USF34-4507-E, *Arthur Rothstein*; Badlands of SD, May, 1936. **2** LC USF33-6649-M3, *Ben Shahn*; New Carlisle, OH, summer, 1938. **3** LC USF34-9667-E, *Dorothea Lange*.

Pages 48-49: **1** LC USF34-4052-E, *Arthur Rothstein*; Cimarron County, OK, 1936. **2** LC USZ62-47353; Elkhart, KS, May, 1937. **3** LC USF34-4085-E, *Rothstein*; Oklahoma, Apr., 1936. **4** USDA-SCS COLO-300; Baca County, CO, 1938. **5** NRECA, *Sloan* (a Soil Conservation Service photo, but USDA has no negative); O.N. Olsen farm. Gregory County, SD, May 13, 1936.

Pages 50-51: **1** LC USF34-2485-D, *Arthur Rothstein*; Texas panhandle, Mar., 1936. **2** LC USF33-11122-M1, *Russell Lee*: Glen Cook family, Woodbury County, IA, Dec., 1936. **3** LC USF34-43859-D, *Jack Delano*; Franklin, GA, Apr., 1941. **4** TVA Kx424 (NRECA); Knox County, TN, 1939.

Pages 52-53: **1** *The Des Moines Register*, P.O. Box 957, Des Moines, IA 50304 (courtesy *Rural America*, 1302 18th St., N.W. #302, Washington, DC 20036, from Iowa History and Archives collection). **2** *The Des Moines Register*, courtesy ISU, *In No Time at All*. **3** LC USF344-3717-ZB, *Russell Lee*; 1937. **4** *The Des Moines Register, George Yates* (courtesy Rural America, address above); National Guard at farm auction, Crawford, IA, Apr. 4, 1933.

Pages 54-55: **1** LC USF34-44563-D, *Jack Delano*; Green County, GA, Jun., 1941. **2** LC USF34-16676-C, *Dorothea Lange*; New Mexico, 1937. **3** LC USF34-18294-C, *Dorothea Lange*; Nettie Featherston, Childress, TX, Jun., 1938. **4** LC USF34-18227-C, *Dorothea Lange*.

Pages 56-57: **1** Life Picture Service, *Margaret Bourke-White*; (copyright 1936 Time, Inc., reproduction forbidden without express consent of Time, Inc.); in Nov. 23, 1936, issue of *Life*; Room 28-58, Time & Life Building, Rockefeller Center, New York, NY 10020. **2** FDR NPx 47-96-1417; owner UPI (Acme) (The Bettmann Archive). **3** FDR NPx 62-128; owner UPI (Acme) (The Bettmann Archive).

Pages 58-59: **1** Nebraska State Historical Society N855-39; 1500 R St., Box 82554, Lincoln, NE 68501. **2** TVA 1030 (NRECA). **3** TVA 1965 (NRECA). **4** TVA H-111 (NRECA). **5** FDR NPx72-37:4; owner UPI (INS) (The Bettmann Archive).

Pages 60-61: **1** REA papers at National Archives (NRECA). **2** & **3** NRECA.

Pages 62-63: **1** NRECA. **2** FDR NPx 49-164:1992(31); owner Wide World Photos.

Pages 64-65: **1** NRECA, drawing by *Socorro Q. Gonzalez*. **2** NA 221-G-694. **3** NA 33-SC-13399; Montgomery County, MD, 1930. **4** USDA, BN-38966; Thompson farm, Montgomery County, MD, Aug., 1930. **5** & **6** NRECA, Pioneer EC.

Pages 66-67: **1** NRECA. **2** *George W. Norris*, by Norman Zucker, University of Illinois Press, Urbana, 1966. **3** U.S. Senate Historian's Office 17A-18. **4** Lyndon B. Johnson Library 34135-13-6C; Austin, TX 78705. **5** NRECA, drawing by *Barba-*

ra L. Gibson.

Pages 68-69: **1** & **5** Norris, 1930 campaign broadside (NRECA). **2** NA 221-G-4604. **3** U.S. Postal Service. **4** Nebraska State Historical Society N855-43a; 1500 R St., Box 82554, Lincoln, NE 68501.

Pages 70-71: **1** NRECA. **2** USDA BN-50735. **3** NA 221-G-377. **4** USDA BN-50740 (also NA 221-G-593).

Pages 72-73: **1** NA 221-G-1289. **2** FDR NPx79-130(1) (may also be in REA collection at NA). **3** REA, *1938 Annual Report* (NRECA). **4** NA 221-G-2341.

Pages 74-75: **1** & **2** REA, *1937 Annual Report* (NRECA). **3** NA 221-G-592. **4** USDA BN-46081.

Pages 76-77: **1** FDR NPx 57-69(3); owner UPI (Acme) (The Bettmann Archive). **2** NA 221-G-2527. **3** NA 221-G-2599. **4** NRECA (probably also in REA collection at NA). **5** FDR NPx48-22:3710(247); owner UPI (Acme) (The Bettmann Archive). **6** FDR NPx53-227(55) (probably also in REA collection at NA).

Page 78: NRECA

Pages 80-81: **1** LC USF34-60927-D, *John Vachon*; Granger Homestead, IA, Apr., 1940. **2** NA 221-G-662. **3** Courtesy *Marshall Gall*; Herried, SD, circa 1912. **4** State Historical Society of Wisconsin WHi(W6)27011; Alva Paddock farm, Kenosha County, WI; 816 State St., Madison, WI 53706.

Pages 82-83: **1** USDA BN-50747 (also NA 221-G-9196); Tyndall, SD, Apr., 1945. **2** LC USF33-3332-M4, *Arthur Rothstein*; Central Iowa 4-H Club Fair, Marshalltown, IA, Sep., 1939.

Pages 84-85: **1** NA 221-G-438. **2** NRECA, Pioneer EC. **3** USDA BN-46954 (also probably NA 221-G-6937-D). **4** USDA BN-50741 (also NA 221-G-2507). **5** LC USF34-64698, *John Vachon*; Farmers Union meeting, Williston, ND, Feb., 1942. **6** NA 221-G-1735.

Pages 86-87: **1** NA 221-G-8759; Illini EC, Champaign-Urbana, IL, Apr., 1945. **2** LC USF34-60607-D, *John Vachon*; Grundy County, IA, Apr., 1940. **3** NA 221-G-299. **4** NRECA.

Pages 88-89: **1-3**, **5** *Friday* magazine, Apr. 25, 1941 (NRECA). **4** & **6** NRECA (from NA).

Pages 90-91: **1** USDA BN-34791. **2** NA 221-G-8643. **3** USDA BN-50742 (also probably NA 221-G-1869). **4** NA 221-G-8647. **5** NRECA; Norton Falls, KS, 1948.

Pages 92-93: **1** USDA BN-50751, *J.W. McManigal* (also NA 221-G-2343A). **2** NA 221-G-139. **3** ISU, *In No Time At All* (courtesy *Farm Town, A Memoir of the 1930s*), *J.W. McManigal* (NRECA) (this photo has been lost from the REA collection). **4** NA 221-G-140.

Pages 94-95: **1** NA 221-G-7533. **2** NA 221-G-7395, *Monte Montague*. **3** NA 221-G-9271. **4** NRECA. **5** NA 221-G-1852. **6** NA 221-G-469. **7** NA 221-G-470.

Pages 96-97: **1** REA, *Rural Electrification News*, Jan., 1939 (NRECA). **2** REA, *Rural Electrification News*, Feb. 1939 (NRECA). **3** NA 221-G-3178. **4** NA 221-G-2134.

Pages 98-99: **1** NRECA, Basin Electric Power Cooperative. **2** NA 221-G-4148-A. **3** USDA BN-50744 (also NA 221-G-2329).

Pages 100 - 101: **1** TVA K-189 (NRECA). **2** REA, *A Guide for Members of REA Cooperatives*, 1940 (NRECA). **3** TVA K-466 (NRECA). **4** NRECA, Hancock-Wood EC. **5** NA 33-SC-13487, *G.W. Ackerman*; home of Mrs. G.M. Thompson, Oneco, FL, 1930. **6** LC USF34-32188-D, *Russell Lee*; Feb., 1939.

Pages 102-103: **1** TVA Kx 2580 (NRECA). **2** TVA 1192 (NRECA). **3** LC USF33-12098-M1, *Russell Lee*; Ernest Milton farm, El Indio, TX, Mar., 1939. **4** NA 16-N-1613, *Forsythe*. **5** NA 221-G-352. **6** NA 221-G-7560. **7** NA 221-G-674. **8** NRECA; Arkansas. **9** NRECA; Arkansas. **10** LC USZ62-83172. **11** USDA BN-50749 (also probably NA 221-G-8420).

Pages 104-105: **1** LC USW3-3901-D, *Arthur Rothstein*; Jun., 1942. **2** REA, *A Guide for Members of REA Cooperatives*, 1940 (NRECA). **3** LC USZ62-83180. **4** LC USZ62-83181. **5** USDA 0975R1950-28.

Pages 106-107: **1** NA 221-G-8876. **2** NA 33-S-3548. **3** Harbutt/Archives, Archive Pictures Inc., 111 Wooster St. (5E), New York, NY 10012. **4** NA 33-SC-6441. **5** LC USW3-6452-D, *Arthur Rothstein*; Aug., 1942. **6** NA 145-AAA-7528W; Mrs. Mark Brown. **7** TVA K2089 (NRECA).

Pages 108-109: **1** TVA Kx 2910 (NRECA). **2** LC USW3-6450-D, *Arthur Rothstein*; Aug., 1942. **3** NA 221-G-4728. **4** NA 221-G-30. **5** NA 221-G-4709.

Pages 110-111: **1** NA 33-SC-6714. **2** NA 33-SC-16212. **3** LC USW3-1107-D, *Jack Delano*; Minnesota, Mar., 1942. **4** LC USW3-17304, *John Collier*; Penasco, NM, Jan., 1943. **5** NA 33-SC-7282. **6** NA 221-G-1314. **7** NA 33-SC-14524.

Pages 112-113: **1** USDA-REA (NRECA). **2** LC USF34-44552-D, *Jack Delano*. **3** NA 221-G-8095; Jun., 1941. **4** NA 221-G-10057. **5** *Worthington Daily Globe*, Worthington, MN, Mar. 7, 1977, *Bob Artley*. **6** NA 221-G-10561.

Pages 114-115: **1** & **3** WDAY, Fargo, ND. **2** & **6** ISU, *Farm Broadcasting, The First Sixty Years*, by John C. Baker. **4** USDA BN-15869. **5** NRECA, Sheridan County EC. **7** WHO, Des Moines, IA.

Pages 116-117: **1** & **2** Wide World Photos (AP). **3** Warner Brothers Films, through Memory Shop, 109 East 12th St., New York, NY 10003. **4** Wide World Photos (AP). **5** Culver Pictures, Inc., 660 First Ave., New York, NY 10016. **6** Wide World Photos (AP). **7** FDR NPx47-96:1783.

Pages 118-119: **1** NA 221-G-11010. **2** NA 221-G-6645. **3** NA 221-G-2902. **4** NA 221-G-3844. **5** NA 221-G-6366. **6** USDA BN-50746 (also probably NA 221-G-4521). **7** NA 221-G-1902. **8** USDA BN-50750 (also NA 221-G-6551).

Pages 120-121: **1** & **2** NRECA. **3** TVA H-24 (NRECA). **4** NA 221-G-2328. **5** NA 221-G-1868. **6** NA 221-G-8967. **7** NRECA. **8** NA 83-G-41244-BAE.

Pages 122-123: **1** LC USF34-63244-D, *John Vachon*. **2** NRECA. **3** LC USF34-40792-D, *Jack Delano*.

Pages 124-125: **1** NA 33-SC-3619, *G.W. Ackerman*; New Hartford, NY, Aug., 1938. **2** NA 221-G-5085. **3** NRECA, Marias River EC. **4** TVA Kx2237 (NRECA). **5** LC USF33-1112, *John Vachon*; Halifax, NC, Apr., 1938.

Pages 126-127: **1** & **2** *Courier-Journal* and *Louisville Times*, Louisville, KY 40202. **3** REA, *Rural Electrification News*, Nov., 1938 (NRECA). **4** NRECA, Otsego EC.

Pages 128-129: **1** NRECA. **2** NA 221-G-6316. **3** NA 221-G-6298. **4** NRECA. **5** NRECA, Hancock-Wood EC. **6-8** NRECA, Sheridan-Johnson REA. **9** USDA BN-43874.

Pages 130-131: **1** TVA (NRECA). **2** TVA K-1663 (NRECA). **3** LC USF34-41790-D, *Jack Delano*; Presque Isle, ME, Oct., 1940.

Page 132: LC USW3-6444-D, *Arthur Rothstein*; Aug., 1942.

Pages 134-135: **1** NA 221-G-4835. **2** NA 221-G-7489. **3** NA 221-G-4877. **4** NA 221-G-7488. **5** NA 221-G-4925.

Pages 136-137: **1** NRECA, Pacific Northwest Generating Co., *Kenneth McCandless*. **2** NA 221-G-8850. **3** NA 221-G-4985. **4** NA 221-G-432. **5** NA 83-G-44521-BAE. **6** USDA BN-50748 (also NA 221-G-42). **7** NA 221-G-452. **8** NRECA, Beauregard EC. **9** LC USF33-

12149-M1, *Russell Lee*; San Augustine, TX, Apr., 1939. **10** REA, *Rural Electrification News*, Oct. 1938 (NRECA). **11** NA 221-G-11667. **12** REA, *Rural Electrification News*, Oct. 1938 (NRECA). **13** USDA BN-50745 (also NA 221-G-5257).

Pages 138-139: **1** NRECA, Hancock-Wood EC. **2** NA 221-G-8942, *Monte Montague*. **3** NA 221-G-3228. **4** NA 221-G-10979. **5** NA 221-G-8912, *Montague*.

Pages 140-141: **1** NRECA. **2** NA 221-G-7786. **3** NA 221-G-10355. **4** NRECA. **5** NRECA, Golden Valley EA. **6** NRECA, Southside EC. **7** NRECA, courtesy of *Mrs. Hayden A. Cox*. **8** NRECA.

Pages 142-143: **1** NRECA. **2** LC USW3-6309-D, *Arthur Rothstein*. **3** NA-16-N-1566, *Forsythe*. **4** NA 221-G-9035. **5** NRECA, *Rural Louisiana, Whitney Belanger*. **6** LC USW3-3945-D, *Rothstein*. **7** NRECA, Clark REC.

Pages 144-145: **1** *The Courier-Journal* and *The Louisville Times*, Louisville, KY 40202. **2** *Lewiston* (ID) *Tribune* (NRECA). **3** NA 221-G-5926. **4** NA 221-G-3188. **5-6** NRECA. **7** & **8** NRECA, *Rural Louisiana, Whitney Belanger*. **9** NRECA. **10** NA 221-G-9267. **11** BPA (NRECA).

Pages 146-147: **1** NRECA, Pacific Northwest Generating Co., *Kenneth McCandless*. **2** NRECA. **3** NA 221-G-8641. **4** USDA BN-50743 (also NA 221-G-7785). **5** NRECA. **6** NRECA, Carroll EC. **7** NRECA, Lumbee River EMC. **8** NRECA, *Wisconsin REC News*. **9** NA 221-G-1674.

Pages 148-149: **1** NRECA, *Rural Arkansas*. **2** TVA (NRECA). **3** NRECA, Scott-New Madrid-Mississippi EC.

Pages 150-151: **1** TVA Kx 2803 (NRECA). **2** NRECA, *Rural Arkansas*. **3** NRECA, Sioux Valley Empire EA. **4** NRECA, Alabama REA. **5** NRECA, Pioneer EC. **6** & **7** NRECA. **8** NRECA, Southeastern Michigan REC. **9** & **10** NRECA.

Pages 152-153: **1** NRECA, Chugach EC. **2** NRECA, Scott-New Madrid-Mississippi EC. **3** NA 221-G-2575. **4** NRECA, Eastern Iowa L&P. **5** NRECA, Ninnescah RECA. **6** NRECA, Davie EMC. **7** NRECA, Southside EC. **8** NRECA, Pearl River Valley EPA. **9** TVA Kx2761 (NRECA).

Pages 154-155; All except photo no 3: NRECA, Belmont EC. **3** USDA BN-44665.

Pages 156-157: **1** NA 221-G-5238. **2** NA 221-G-5995. **3** NRECA, Belmont EC. **4** NA 221-G-5237. **5** NA 221-G-5235.

Pages 158-159: **1** Courtesy *Arthur Rothstein*; Pittsburgh, 1936. **2** LC USW3-6625-D, *Rothstein*. **3** LC USW3-6597-D, *Rothstein*. **4** LC USW3-6639-D, *Rothstein*.

Pages 160-161: All LC photos by *Arthur Rothstein*. **1** USW3-6689-D. **2** USW3-6611-D. **3** USW3-6558-D. **4** USW3-6561-D. **5** USW3-6614-D. **6** USW3-6654-D.

Pages 162-163: All LC photos by *Arthur Rothstein*. **1** USW3-6580-D. **2** USW3-6592-D. **3** USW3-6564-D.

Pages 164-165: All NA photos by *Estelle Campbell*. **1** 221-G-7149. **2** 221-G-7152. **3** 221-G-7151. **4** 221-G-7155. **5** 221-G-7154. **6** 221-G-7150. **7** NA- 221-G-7145.

Pages 166-167: **1** NA 221-G-7435. **2** BPA (NRECA). **3** BPA (NRECA). **4** NA 221-G-7675. **5** NA 221-G-7678. **6** NA 221-G-7665. **7** REA, *Rural Electrification News*, Jun., 1944 (NRECA). **8** NA 221-G-7580. **9** Wide World Photos (AP). **10** The George Arents Research Library, Syracuse University, Syracuse, NY 13210. **11** NA 221-G-6138. **12** Missouri Historical Society, Jefferson Memorial Building, Forest Park, St. Louis, MO 63112.

Pages 168-169: **1** Courtesy *Irlene Lewis Hess*. **2** Missouri Historical Society; from the *St. Louis Star-Times*, Mar. 27, 1942. **3** NA 221-G-7339, *Estelle Campbell*. **4** Courtesy *Irlene Lewis Hess*. **5** Courtesy *Irlene Lewis Hess* (photo by *Estelle Campbell*; also probably in REA collection at NA). **6** NA 221-G-7294. **7** NA 221-G-7135. **8** NA 221-G-7495.

Pages 170-171: All photos available from NRECA, courtesy Maquoketa Valley REC; some of these photos also are possibly in the REA collection at NA, perhaps under these numbers: **2** 221-G-7598. **3** 221-G-7602. **4** 221-G-7604. **7** 221-G-7616.

Pages 172-173: **1** NA 221-G-7299, *Jim Weeks*. **2** NA 221-G-8740, *Monte Montague*. **3** LC USF33-3332-M5, *Arthur Rothstein*. **4** LC USF34-5298-A, *Rothstein*. **5** Life Picture Service (copyright 1945 Time, Inc., reproduction forbidden without express consent of Time, Inc.), *Edward Clark*; Room 28-58, Time & Life Building, Rockefeller Center, New York, NY 10020.

Pages 174-175: SONJ 8374, *Sol Libsohn*.

Pages 176-177: **1** NA 221-G-8628. **2** NA 221-G-8972. **3** NA 221-G-8328, *Monte Montague*. **4** SONJ 54606, *John Vachon*; Ransom County, ND. **5** NA 221-G-8483. **6** NA 221-G-8941. **7** REA poster (NRECA).

Pages 178-179: **1-4** NRECA. **5** NA 221-G-9742, *Monte Montague*. **6** TVA 16900-1, *E. O. Romska*; courtesy American Public Power Association (NRECA).

Pages 180-181: **1** BPA (NRECA). **2-4** NRECA . **5** Life Picture Service (copyright 1937 Time, Inc., reproduction forbidden without express consent of Time, Inc.), *Margaret Bourke-White*; Room 28-58, Time & Life Building, Rockefeller Center, New York, NY 10020. **6** BPA (NRECA). **7** Bureau of Reclamation, *F. B. Pomeroy* (NRECA). **8** Bureau of Reclamation (NRECA).

Pages 182-183: **1** NRECA, Brazos Electric Power Cooperative. **2** NRECA, *Texas Co-op Power*. **3** NRECA, East Kentucky Power Co-op. **4** NRECA, Central Power Electric Co-op. **5** NRECA, Dairyland Power Cooperative. **6** NRECA, Corn Belt Power Co-op. **7** NRECA, Corn Belt. **8** NA 221-G-7487.

Pages 184-185: **1** NRECA, Eastern Iowa L&P. **2** NRECA, Cooperative Power Association. **3** & **4** NRECA. **5** NRECA, courtesy of Iowa Electric Light & Power Co. **6** NRECA. **7** USDA BN-32597. **8** NRECA. **9** NRECA, Basin Electric Power Cooperative.

Pages 186-187: All photos NRECA, United Power Association.

Pages 188-189: **1-4** NRECA. **5** NRECA, *Sharon O'Malley*. **6** REA (NRECA). **7** NRECA. **8** REA (NRECA). **9** NRECA, *Frank Gallant*. **10** NRECA, *Tom Hoy*.

Page 190: NRECA.

Pages 192-193: **1** NRECA, Amicalola EMC, courtesy Mrs. Steve Tate. **2** NRECA, *Wisconsin REC News*. **3** NRECA. **4** NRECA, Anoka EC. **5** NRECA. **6** NRECA, *Rural Arkansas*. **7** NRECA, *Leet Brothers*, Washington, DC. **8** NRECA, Central Electric Power Cooperative. **9** NRECA, *Cristof Studio*, San Francisco, CA. **10** NRECA, Tri-County EC. **11** NRECA. **12** NRECA, *Day Photographers*, St. Louis, MO. **13** NRECA. **14** NRECA, *Day Photographers*. **15** NA 221-G-7283. **16** NA 221-G-4525.

Pages 194-195: All NRECA; **2** *Fabian Bachrach*.

Pages 196-197: **1** Mid-West Electric Consumers Association, *Mid-West News* (NRECA). **2** NRECA. **3** USDA (NRECA). **4** NRECA. **5** Wide World Photos (AP). **6** & **7** NRECA.

Pages 198-199: **1-5** NRECA. **6** USDA-REA (NRECA).

Pages 200-201: All NRECA.

Pages 202-203: All NRECA.

Pages 204-205: **1** *Arkansas Gazette*, Little Rock (NRECA). **2-4** NRECA. **5** NRECA, Adams EC.

Pages 206-207: **1 & 2 NRECA. 3** NRECA, *Raymond Kuhl*. **4** NRECA. **5 & 7** NRECA, *Texas Co-op Power*. **6** NA 221-G-4613. **8 & 9** NRECA.

Pages 208-209: **1** USDA-REA (NRECA). **2-6** NRECA.

Pages 210-211: All NRECA. **4** *Schawang Photo*, St. Paul, MN.

Pages 212-213: **1** NRECA, *Cristof Studio*, San Francisco. **2-5** NRECA. **6** NA 221-G-8114. **7** NRECA. **8** NRECA, *Robert Gibson*.

Pages 214-215: All pictures NRECA; **2** courtesy Planters EMC.

Pages 216-217: **1-5** NRECA. **6** NRECA, *The Carolina Farmer, Richard A. Pence*. **7** NRECA. **8** Folkway Records & Service Corp., 43 West 61st St., New York NY 10023. **9** Woody Guthrie Publications, 250 West 57th St., Suite 2017, New York, NY 10019. **10 & 11** NRECA.

Pages 218-219: All photos NRECA. **2** cartoon by *Andrew L McLay*.

Pages 220-221: **1** NRECA. **2** World Bank (NRECA). **3** NRECA. **4** United States Information Agency (NRECA). **5** USIA (NRECA). **6 & 7** NRECA.

Pages 222-223: All NRECA.

Pages 224-225: NRECA; all cartoons by *Web Allison*; photo courtesy *Allison*.

Pages 226-227: **1-3** NRECA. **4** NRECA, *Web Allison*. **5 & 6** NRECA, National Rural Utilities Cooperative Finance Corporation. **7** NRECA.

Pages 228-229: **1** NRECA (probably in REA collection at NA). **2** USDA, *Mitchell* (NRECA). **3** NRECA, Vermont EC. **4** USDA-REA (NRECA). **5** NRECA. **6** USDA-REA (NRECA). **7** USDA-REA (NRECA).

Pages 230-231: **1** NRECA. **2-4** USDA-REA (NRECA), courtesy *Norman M. Clapp*. **5** USDA-REA (NRECA). **6** NRECA. **7** REA (NRECA). **8** NRECA. **9** USDA-REA (NRECA). **10** NRECA.

Pages 232-233: **1-5** NRECA. **6** REA (NRECA), courtesy *Harold V. Hunter*. **7** NRECA. **8** REA (NRECA). **9** REA (NRECA). **10** REA (NRECA). **11** NRECA, *South Dakota High Liner, Martin McGrane*.

Pages 234-235: **1-7** NRECA. **8** NRECA, *Sharon O'Malley*. **9** NRECA, *Robert Gibson*. **10 & 11** NRECA.

Page 236: Cajun Electric Power Co-op, P.O. Box 15540, Baton Rouge, LA 70895.

Pages 238-239: **1, 3, 4, 5, 6, 8, 9 & 10** NRECA, *Robert Gibson*. **2** USDA HOG-0-54. **7** USDA Dairy-Calves.

Pages 240-241: **1** USDA Sheep-Flock-0-19. **2 & 3** NRECA, *Robert Gibson*. **4** USDA 3-18. **5 & 6** USDA. **7** NRECA, *Gibson*. **8** USDA.

Pages 242-243: **1** Cobb EMC, P.O. Box 369, Marietta, GA 30061. **2 & 3** NRECA, *Robert Gibson*. **4** Basin Electric Power Cooperative, 1717 Interstate Ave., Bismarck, ND 58501. **5** NRECA, *Gibson*. **6** Honda Motor Company, Marysville, OH. **7** Indiana Statewide Association of REC, P.O. Box 24517, Indianapolis, IN 46224; *Mike Hanley*. **8** U.S. Naval Air Station, Patuxent, MD.

Pages 244-245: **1 & 6** Basin Electric Power Cooperative. **2** Indiana Statewide, *Mike Hanley*. **3** Big Rivers Electric Corp. **4 & 5** Cooperative Power Association. **7** NRECA, *Robert Gibson*.

Page 246: (Except for photo **2**, the photos on this page and pages 248 and 250 were among the first photographs taken using Eastman-Kodak's new Ektachrome 35-mm film; only a few of these have ever been published.) **1** LC USF351-330, *Russell Lee*; Pie Town, NM, Oct., 1940. **2** TVA, Wilson Dam mural (order from TVA, Knoxville, TN). **3** LC USF351-373, *Russell Lee*, Pie Town, NM, Oct., 1940.

Page 248: **1** LC USF351-268, *John Vachon*, Lincoln, NE. **2** LC USF351-319, *Russell Lee*, Jack Whinery and family, Pie Town, NM, 1940. **3** LC USF35-192, *Marion Post Wolcott*; Campton, KY, Sep., 1940.

Page 250: **1** LC USF351-114, *Marion Post Wolcott*; Schriever, LA, Jun., 1940. **2** LC USF35-33, *Jack Delano*; Derby, CN, Sep., 1940. **3** LC USF35-272, *John Vachon*; Junction City, KS.

BIBLIOGRAPHY

Following is a list of publications consulted extensively during the production of this book. Those available are recommended for further reading.

Brown, D. Clayton, *Electricity for Rural America: The Fight for REA*, Greenwood Press, 1980

Childs, Marquis W., *Yesterday, Today and Tomorrow: The Farmer Takes a Hand*, NRECA, Washington, DC, 1980

Cooke, Morris L., Administrator, REA, "The Early Days of the Rural Electrification Idea," *The American Political Science Review*, June 1948

Cooper, Donald H., former information officer, REA, and former NRECA research specialist, private papers

Coyle, David Cushman, *Conservation: An American Story of Conflict and Accomplishment*, Rutgers University Press, 1957

Funigiello, Philip J., *Toward a National Power Policy: The New Deal and the Electric Utility Industry, 1933-1941*, University of Pittsburgh Press, 1973

Knapp, Joseph G., *The Advance of American Cooperative Enterprise: 1920-1945*, The Interstate Publishers, 1973

Kramer, Dale, *The Wild Jackasses: The American Farmer In Revolt*, Hastings House, 1956

Mamer, Louisan, former home economist, member relations specialist and one of the first employees, REA, private papers

Norwood, Gus, *Columbia River Power for the People: A History of the Policies of the Bonneville Power Administration*, BPA, Portland, OR, 1980

Partridge, Robert Darwin, *Governmental Assistance In Rural Electrification - Its objectives, Accomplishments and Significance*, unpublished master of arts thesis, American University, Washington, DC, 1955

Person, H.S., management consultant, REA, "The Rural Electrification Administration In Perspective," *Agricultural History* (quarterly journal), April 1950

Pinchot, Gifford, *Breaking New Ground*, Harcourt Brace and Company, 1947

Rall, Udo, cooperative specialist, REA, unpublished recollections of cooperative rural electrification

Richardson, Truman, *The Norris-Rayburn Act of 1936*, unpublished legislative history, December 1958

Rosenman, Samuel I., *The Public Papers and Addresses of Franklin D. Roosevelt*, Random House, 1938

REA, *Rural Electrification News, Rural Lines* (official monthly publications), and *Rural Lines USA: The Story of the Rural Electrification Administration's First Twenty-Five Years* (Publication No. 811), Government Printing Office, Washington, DC

Slattery, Harry, Administrator, REA, *Rural America Lights Up*, National Home Library Foundation, Washington, DC, 1956

Smith, Frank E., *The Politics of Conservation*, Pantheon Books, 1956

Trombley, Kenneth E., *The Life and Times of a Happy Liberal: A Biography of Morris Llewellyn Cooke*, Harper and Roe, 1954

363.6
PEN

Pence, Richard

The Next Greatest thing

DATE	ISSUED TO

Clay County Public Library
116 Guffey Street
Celina, TN 38551
(931) 243-3442